NOEL MACKLIN

FROM INVICTA AND RAILTON TO THE FAIRMILE BOATS

NOEL MACKLIN

FROM INVICTA AND RAILTON TO THE FAIRMILE BOATS

DAVID THIRLBY

TEMPUS

Front cover: **Noel Macklin, painted by Keith Woodcock.**

Frontispiece: Noel Macklin from a studio portrait, taken during the Second World War, and presented to 'Cushie' Cushman.

Previously Published
The Chain Drive Frazer Nash – MacDonalds, 1965
Frazer Nash – Haynes, 1977
Frazer Nash 1923–1957 – Thirlby Publicity, 2000
Minimal Motoring – Tempus Publishing Ltd, 2002

First published 2006

Tempus Publishing Limited
The Mill, Brimscombe Port,
Stroud, Gloucestershire, GL5 2QG
www.tempus-publishing.com

British Library Cataloguing in Publication Data.
A catalogue record for this book is available from the British Library.

ISBN 0 7524 3879 4

Typesetting and origination by Tempus Publishing Limited
Printed in Great Britain

CONTENTS

ACKNOWLEDGEMENTS

This writer was asked in 2001 by Ian and Marian Rendall of the Invicta Car Club to write a history of Invicta. This came about since the Rendalls knew that my writings on the marque Frazer Nash were complete and that I was no longer editor of the *Vintage Sports-Car Club Bulletin*. Without the Rendalls' help this book would have been very much underwritten.

The motoring historian whose help I sought was Michael Worthington-Williams, who on a number of occasions put me right, and his information on the Black Prince transmission was splendid. The same comment has to apply to the various members of the Vintage Sports-Car Club I approached, and typical of these was Bernard Harding who researched the topography of Cobham and the local council archives. Nic Walker, the librarian of the VSCC, dealt very promptly with my enquiries.

Various members of the Macklin family were extremely helpful – in particular Sally Harrison, who is Violette Cordery's daughter and who had lived in the Lodge facing on to the Fairmile main road as a child. I enjoyed meeting Paddy Macklin and Miranda Kelly, granddaughters of Sir Noel, and especially Shelagh Montague-Browne, who had been married to Lance Macklin and was the mother of Paddy and Miranda. Bunty Van Dyne, who appears in the story as Bunty Macklin, was splendid. But there is a well known caveat – one should not rely on the memories of family members when dealing with commercial matters. Heroes can have a dual facility when the two aspects of family and business are considered. His kindness to others was common both to home and business life. I only met one person who had known Noel Macklin through a day-to-day business connection – Betty Metchim, who had been a draughtswoman on the Fairmile during the war – and she was in her ninety-third year when I met her.

The photographs that members of the family provided led me to ice hockey and the Cresta. Martin Harris filled in this part of the story and introduced Lady Brabazon of Tara for the Cresta Run details. A.H. Fraser-Mitchell of the Handley Page Association supplied the information on Beans, and that was supplemented by motoring historian Johnathan Wood for the Eric Campbell component, and John Harrison of the Swift Club. Jeremy Wood was very helpful with Eric Campbell documentation.

There were no factory records of car production, with the exception of the Railton. The only car which members of the various Invicta clubs over the years had sought to record, before this century, was the S-Type. Derek Green started me off on Invicta history and Duncan MacGregor filled in.

Unfortunately through all the years very little had been done to interview the personnel who worked for the Noel Macklin companies – Douglas Irvine had interviewed two of the fitters, but there were no records of meetings with Noel Macklin or the next most important person – 'Cushie' Cushman. Since the writer knew 'Cushie' during the 1950s, this made the meeting with his son, who was an astonishing replica of his father, in speech and attitude, that much easier. Mrs Pam Gregory, as the daughter of William Watson, had some memories.

The only really positive help was from all the 'notes' that Michael Sedgwick had gathered together for the splendid book *Lost Causes of Motoring* (1960), which contained one chapter on Invicta and Railton, entitled 'Rivets down the bonnet'. He had presented his 'notes' to the Invicta Club, which were mainly in the form of copies of letters he had written and the replies received. Michael Sedgwick did not usually interview people, but conducted postal questionnaires – this has obvious drawbacks because the person questioned could reply with a response that was not sought – in the manner of politicians. There was one exception to this – he lived reasonably close to Gladys Starkey, who had been at the Fairmile from the very beginning and was still there in the post-1945 period. The 'notes' were lent to this author by Andrew Crisford. This author soon decided that the book had to be a biography of Noel Macklin, rather than just the story of the Invicta.

Lance Macklin, Noel's only son, wrote his version of the Macklin family history, which has to be a guide only, as most of the family papers were destroyed in what has been reported as a burglary/fire in Spain. Nevertheless, the chapter on the Macklin family comes mainly from his writings, as does the Monte Carlo story. Hamish Orr-Ewing, the son of Hugh Orr-Ewing, helped with his memories of what his father had told him. Reid Railton fortunately kept copies of all his correspondence, and his widow made these available to the Railton Owners Club (celebrating their fiftieth anniversary) and the Railton story was made easier due to this. Peter Baines of the Rolls-Royce Enthusiasts Club made available the Rolls-Royce company notes as they pertained to Railton. The Fack brothers, John Dyson, and Nigel Plant were invaluable Railton advisers. Sally Joslin, Reid Railton's daughter, lives in Boston, USA, and she filled in some of the material of the Fairmile story.

The Fairmile boat story came out of an article published by Vice Admiral Usborne and the copy that fellow Vintage Sports Car Club member and wartime RNVR lieutenant Bob Fletcher in Coastal Defence provided. David Holland offered a Vosper insight. Tom Cunningham has also proofread many of these pages from his knowledge of the RNVR and he has my sincere thanks. The post-war, post-Noel Macklin, chapter could be regarded as an addendum, but it is part of the story and Michael Bristow welcomed me to the Chippenham works where the Invicta S1 was being made. The story of the Invicta post-1945 was necessary to complete the life and works of Noel Macklin.

Although the author has made every effort to attain permission to reproduce the extracts appearing on pages 76–81 and 131–133, this was, sadly, not possible as both authors are now deceased and the publishers are no longer in business.

My thanks to Alan Cox and David Venables, assistant editors in my *VSCC Bulletin* days, who both proofread a lot of my published works in the past and were again all-important for this book. David Venables researched the Army career of Noel Macklin and set me on the right path in other sections. Proofreading this page shows to me, the author, the enormous debt I owe to the people above, whose help was all-embracing, and so many of them are members of the Vintage Sports Car Club.

David Thirlby
Northwich, Cheshire

PREFACE

Noel Macklin's character shone like a beacon to all who knew him. He was quiet, kind, very considerate and a listener. He would never dismiss anybody's suggestions out of hand, but would always say he would like to consider their point of view, and would often come back many days later with a variant of what had been said, which he always acknowledged as the other person's idea. When he came head-to-head with an equally strong personality, such as Reid Railton, this could have led to wrong decisions being made. Railton would ask for Macklin to put his ideas on paper which Railton could then contemplate, without Macklin's strong personality intruding on his own decision-making process. Noel Macklin was a brilliant businessman who left no enemies in his wake – his difficult times were when he considered that a business had run its course and fierce decisions had to be made.

Noel Macklin was short in stature, but this was never obvious and, as his grandson said, 'all Macklins are on the short side'. His whole style made him very attractive to women, with whom he was inordinately successful.

A WORD PICTURE OF NOEL MACKLIN BY NADA CARAMAN
(NOEL MACKLIN'S DAUGHTER)

I was born in Bramham Square, Kensington, in November 1917, where my parents had a house. The houses were tall and narrow and backed onto a large garden used by all the occupants of the Square. My brother Lance and sister Mia were both born there during the next three years. In about 1922 we moved to Glengariff on the Wisley road out of Cobham in Surrey. In 1925 we moved to the Fairmile on the London road into Cobham. We moved because the house and outbuildings were larger and there were nine acres of ground in total. The kitchen garden contained small animals; when we moved in there were two pigs, ducks, chickens, turkeys and two goats. The grounds included three smaller properties, the Entrance Lodge, a gardeners' cottage and a chauffeur's cottage. There was a head gardener for flowers – Gullick, a kitchen gardener – Randall, and two boys that helped.

The house itself had nine bedrooms and five staff rooms, which were on the ground floor. The 'nursery wing' was completely separate from the house and was over the kitchen and pantry. We had a nurse, later to be a governess, and two nursery maids to look after us. There was also a cook, a parlour maid, an under parlour maid, three house maids and a 'boot-boy' in the kitchen.

The whole family spent three or four months every year at Menton, close to Monte Carlo, but there again we were mostly kept separate from my parents with our own governess. When I was ten years of age I was allowed down to lunch in the dining room on Sundays!

I remember my father as having very blue eyes and a soft speaking voice and I do not remember him ever getting in a temper with us. He was a good pianist and played very well, usually jazz. He was very active and a good shot. He played cricket, walked a lot and often took us ice skating at Princes on Park Lane on Sunday afternoons. I do not remember him ever riding, but I did know he was an amateur rider before the war. We often went to Sandown Park to watch the racing and he placed bets up until the Second World War.

Father was usually dressed in a very relaxed way with grey flannels and a tweed sports coat with a white or pale blue shirt and usually a light blue tie but he often wore an Old Etonian tie. He had a London tailor and for business wore well cut navy blue suits with a pale blue silk shirt, but generally he was dressed in 'sports clothes'. He was very persuasive with enormous charm. Allied with this he had a great deal of imagination and an enquiring mind, which was always thinking up new projects. He was consistently in advance of his time with new gadgets and we had a television set long before the Second World War.

He smoked heavily, especially Egyptian tobacco, with which cigarettes were hand rolled for him in London, and Harvey, the chauffeur, would go to London once a week to fetch them and then go on to Fortnum and Masons to get pheasant paté, which he loved. He had a silver cigarette case for the daytime (which I still have) and a gold one for the evening. He was a complete teetotaller; there was never any alcohol in the house, which may have been due to the fact that Cecil, his younger brother, was an alcoholic and died young. Father took a house on the Isle of Wight and kept a motor yacht there. At the outbtreak of war we were all in Menton and came home straight away, myself and my fiancé by car and Mia with the parents by the Blue Train.

He refused a salary from the Admiralty when they took over the financing and running of the MTB project, but had to accept a minimum payment of £1 a year and payment of his personal expenses. During the war he took a house close to Oxford so that we could all get away at the weekends from the German bombing run to London. We were bombed several times but there were three large air raid shelters in which we slept.

From about the start of the 1930s he started having bad arthritis in both legs, which got steadily worse and prevented physical activities. During the war years he was finally crippled and died at the end of the war of heart trouble, brought on by the arthritis. Violette Cordery used to look after him and trundle him around the house in a wheelchair and help him get into the car. But his invalidity was only for the family to see. If he went into the Fairmile design offices then he would walk slowly but positively. He did not want people to pity him. In those days the ailment had only recently been separated from rheumatism and though doctors tried 'gold' injections they did not work. Father's chauffeur – Harvey – who was with him before the First World War, got married in Cobham and had two children of whom one was called Nada. He stayed until father's death in 1946. Father was cremated and his ashes were spread close to his own father at Bisham Church on the edge of the Thames.

Noel Macklin's life as an entrepreneur was without doubt the result of inbred characteristics inherited from his family, which included charm, height, and build. No Macklins ever seem to be tall and all are slight in build. He had a brilliant mind, a very special personality, overwhelming charm and was always relaxed. Very easy to get on with and 'no side at all'. He did not know what snobbery meant and everyone who worked with him, from the boy who cleaned the floor to company directors, got on with him very well. He was very 'modern' in his outlook for those times and all young people adored him, because of his sense of humour and easygoing attitude to life.

ONE

THE MACKLINS

The Irish family of the Macklins were descended from the O'Melaglinns, Kings of Meath, who ruled in the fourth century. In the eleventh century, at the time of the Battle of Boyne, Charles O'Melaglinn was born; King William II fought King James III close to Drogheda, and William's victory made Ireland a Protestant country for 100 years. Charles, being a Catholic, lost his lands, and a change of family livelihood was called for. He became a leading actor and changed his name to Macklin. The Sandby brothers set up sketching and painting classes in the 1750s which can be considered the beginnings of the Royal Academy, and at that time it was written that a Sandby was 'the friend of such men as Foote, Churchill, Garrick, Goldsmith, Macklin and others of the same class'. Charles Macklin's last appearance on the stage was on 7 May 1789 (he must have been ninety years old). He played the part of Shylock in *The Merchant of Venice*, which was one of his best-known roles and one for which he was famous. At a crucial moment he suffered a complete mental blackout and had to be helped off the stage. He died in London in 1797. Having risen that morning and rubbed himself down with rum, as was his wont, he put on clean raiment and then returned to bed. Shortly after he was heard shouting 'Let me go, let me go' followed by complete silence. He was buried in the churchyard of the 'Actors' Church', which is St Pauls, Covent Garden. A plaque on the wall commemorates him.

Charles Macklin's only son, John Macklin, was born in 1760 and died 1793. He was certainly a heavy financial burden on his father most of his life. He obtained a job as a writer with the East India Co. and was sent out to Fort St George, India. On the voyage out he gambled away all the money his father

Noel Macklin with his younger brother Cecil and father 'Golden Charles' — so called because of his beautiful soft speaking voice, which was regarded as very persuasive in legal presentations.

had given him and at once started borrowing heavily. Eventually John's debts absorbed nearly all his father's savings. He later returned to England and studied law for two years without success.

In 1825 a Macklin was born who established the Macklin name in law. By 1850 Charles Macklin was practising in Perth, Australia. Albert Noel Campbell Macklin was born in Perth on 28 October 1886, and his younger brother Cecil was born five years later. Noel learned to ride at the age of four and for the whole of his life he was keen on horses. When Noel was ten years of age, the family set off to return to Britain via the USA, as Charles wanted his sons to have a good education. Charles was very shortly to become one of London's best-known barristers. The family lived in Albert Hall Mansion overlooking Kensington Gardens in London. Albert, now known as Noel, went to a crammer and entered Eton in 1899 at the age of thirteen. He left Eton in December 1901, mid-term, at the age of fifteen, before taking School Certificate. He was like all the Macklins — slight in stature, good-looking in a boyish manner, and he may have been ragged or bullied so much that his father took him away. He achieved no scholastic levels, and other than coxing his house boat, left no other record in the Eton file. He consistently wore his Old Etonian tie throughout the whole of his life; he played ice hockey for a combined Old Etonian/Wellington team in 1903, so he bore no ill-will and always had positive thoughts about Eton.

The family moved to Elm Park Gardens in Chelsea where adjoining roofs had their 'vees' filled in at the ends, which provided a safe play area on the roof. Cecil, Noel's younger brother' owned racing pigeons and Noel bought a tiny lion cub which was kept on the roof, quite separately from the pigeons.

The months went past and the lion grew and his voice matured and a big-game hunter, Captain Harcourt, a near neighbour, identified the deep-throated roar as that of a lion. Noel confessed to his father the ownership of the lion, as a local vigilante group was being set up to hunt the animal. He was told to take it by hansom cab to the zoo. Unsurprisingly, no hansom cab would take the lion, and it had to be taken through the streets on foot in the harness by which it had been lowered from the roof. The zoo declined the offer, as they had a sufficient quota of lions, and Noel and the lion, then footsore, had to be taken to a circus on the south side of the Thames in Battersea Park, where fortunately the lion tamer accepted the gift.

Noel's father had sent him to a further crammer so that he could obtain sufficient education to enter the law.

In 1902 he joined the Princes Club in Knightsbridge, London. There were only three artificially frozen indoor rinks in Britain where ice hockey was played – Princes Club in London and the rinks in Manchester and Glasgow. The game was not played in a recognisable form in Britain until 1902/3, and the participants were either Canadian expatriates or the wealthier leisured classes, who had learnt to play in Switzerland during winter sports holidays. Compared to today's game, the rules were in their infancy, with either six or seven players per team, no substitutes, and only rudimentary body protection.

He played at a high level at ice hockey and represented England, later called Great Britain, in the self funded Princes Team in overseas matches in France and Switzerland, between the years 1906–1910. His best season was 1908/9, when he was a successful forward. In the next season he was twice injured, culminating in a broken kneecap in January 1910, which ended his ice hockey career. Noel Macklin had been playing ice hockey for the Princes Team, representing England against France, and was hit on his left kneecap by the flying puck. This did not shatter his patella, the front plate of the kneecap, but probably cracked it. He endeavoured to play ice hockey again during the next few weeks with his knee strapped up beneath his trousers and with a kneecap bandage externally. It was reported by the *Times* that he had injured his right kneecap, but a team photograph shows him with his left knee strapped. The *Times* of 26 January 1910 reported: 'Princes greatly felt the loss of A.N. Macklin... not yet recovered from accident sustained abroad.' He could not play satisfactorily and had to give up. He may have tried alcohol as a palliative, but one thing was certain – he never drank again. Macklin was quite emphatic later about forbidding alcohol on the Fairmile premises. There had to be a facility for Winston Churchill, when he stated that he would like to see the Fairmile boats design and training facilities, to bring his own 'drinking-water' in bottles during the Second World War, which presumably contained a measurable percentage of brandy.

In April 1907 he was commissioned in the Royal Garrison Artillery Battery of the Kent Militia as a lieutenant. His skill at riding horses would have stood him well. The Militia Regiments were the equivalent of the Territorial Army of today, though for the officers there were strong social connections. When the war came he was made a lieutenant in the Royal Horse Artillery, which was the grandest unit of the Royal Artillery.

Some time before the war he borrowed a large sum of money and gambled on the stock exchange in Malaysian rubber shares. He sold out with a clear profit of £50,000 (£½ million in today's terms — he must have borrowed a king's ransom to set the deal up). He married Esmé Stewart in 1911 and they lived in considerable style on Park Lane, with a full retinue of servants — butler, valet, chauffeur and other servants.

Macklin had met Hugh Orr-Ewing in Scotland. As a keen shot he regularly joined house parties in Scotland and it would have been at one of these house parties that he met Esmé Stewart. Noel and Hugh probably met at the house of the McKinnons in Kintyre on shooting holidays. Hugh married Jane McKinnon in 1912 but they divorced in 1916 during the First World War. Hugh had been a regular soldier in the 2nd Black Watch, and during his time in India had served as ADC to the Viceroy.

Noel raced at Brooklands and drove the Fiat Mephistopheles (when fitted with its original engine of 18 litre capacity, rather than the larger Fiat aviation engine which was fitted later) and encouraged Esmé, his wife, to take part. Noel first competed in a Mercedes but it is said that the Mephistopheles had a light, sensitive clutch which would have suited him with a damaged left knee. Esmé Macklin competed in the car at Brooklands.

Noel Macklin had learnt to ride in Australia as a boy and took part in point-to-point races in England. He became keen on entering horses for steeplechase racing. His racing colours — pink with a lilac belt — were registered to him in 1912. A rider trainer, one R.H. Hall, owned a horse called Odor which finished third in the Grand National of 1910. Hall said he would sell it to Macklin if he could have a run with it in the 1911 National, but in the meantime, under Macklin's ownership, it broke its front leg when in the lead at Sandown Park. This so upset Noel Macklin that the accident finished his racing career and he disposed of his 'string' at Lambourn.

Cecil with Noel kitted up ready to go to his 'prepper' to prepare him for Eton.

Above left: Noel with a knee-cap protector. He was the smallest member of the English ice hockey team in Switzerland. He is talking to T.O.M. Sopwith, later to become the well-known aircraft constructor.

Above right: Noel on the Cresta Run in St Moritz in 1910. In 1912 Macklin donated a silver cup for the Junction Handicap Race. It was won outright by Fairchilds MacCarthy in 1955, and he went on to present the same cup as the Fairchilds MacCarthy Cup — for the same competition which still takes place.

He took up cine-photography, with a commercial view to supplementing his expertise with twelve bore and rifle. He went out to Africa and enjoyed big-game hunting — the various stuffed heads of buffalo, antelope, eland and gazelle graced his homes in Cobham after the war. He returned to Africa before the First World War with two packs of hounds on the P&O passenger liner *Kaisar-I-Hind*, of 11,500 tons, which was used on the London–Bombay route. He shot a considerable quantity of professional quality 35mm film on African wildlife, including a rhinoceros charge, which upended him. He returned via Egypt and on 11 February 1914 he took part in a minor race meeting — the second winter meeting of the Khedival Sporting Club of Cairo, racing at Ghezireh. Mr B.A.P. Schreiber's horse, Shoman, was his mount in the last race of the day, where he finished first equal.

On his return to Britain he intended to edit the African wildlife film into a sellable proposition. The First World War intervened and all his films shot in Africa were lost. By this time he was living with Esmé at 46 Queens Gate Terrace, South Kensington.

Above left: Noel, wearing protection on his left knee, playing for England in a match against Germany, which they won, in the 1910 European Nations Champions Cup.

Above right: Esmé Stewart prior to her marriage to Noel Macklin.

Noel enjoying himself in Scotland before the war, wearing his ever-present Old Etonian tie.

Lieutenant Macklin of the Royal Horse Artillery.

The RHA in action – 'The Guns! Thank God the Guns!' From a painting of guns on the Marne by Charles J. Payne ('Snaffles'), the original of which is in the Royal Artillery Museum.

All countries subscribed, with greater or lesser fervency, to a doctrine of war that laid its emphasis upon mobility and manoeuvre and upon the pursuit of swift action. Infantry was chiefly exercised in fire and movement, and artillery in the direct support role – that is to say, shooting at human targets at close range rather than at terrain features over long ranges (both the French and the Germans had long-range siege guns but these were not moveable without excellent roads or a railway line). However, the infantry and artillery, not to mention their still very numerous cavalry comrades, had been instructed in the tedious, immobile, hole-in-the-corner business of trench warfare, and they were not sufficiently psychologically prepared or physically equipped to wage it. There had been plenty of evidence – in conflicts such as the Boer War and the American Civil War – that modern guns, with their greater accuracy, could tie down armies, but this evidence was wholly ignored by the war councils.

The French theory of attack lay in the word *élan*, a quality that they believed the French soldier alone possessed. Yet there were those who disagreed, like the brilliant military writer and critic Captain Mayer, who vehemently attacked Foch, envisaging instead a siege war that would last for years.

The British went to war against the Boers in South Africa in 1899 convinced that their 'parade ground' tactics, which had been so successful against undisciplined and naïve native opponents, were wholly sufficient to defeat a handful of unruly farmers. The flexibility and cunning of the Boer, armed with modern rifles supplied by Germany, showed otherwise.

Above left: Captain Hugh Orr-Ewing of the Black Watch.

Above right: Noel Macklin and William Watson at Brooklands, prior to the First World War.

British infantry were trained to appreciate the value of individual marksmanship and to think little as individuals. Like the Germans, the British introduced a closer liaison between artillery and infantry. The artillery crews were taught the technique of indirect fire, whereby the guns remained out of sight of the enemy and were controlled by forward observers.

Very few military thinkers and observers foresaw infantry being entrenched on both sides and that artillery would become the dominant arm. The French infantry, advancing in their blue coats and red trousers, as their forbears had a hundred years before, proved no match for the German artillery and machine guns and rapidly suffered 300,000 casualties, thereby proving that élan was not enough to bring about victory. Instead of war being fought out in a series of decisive battles, the substitute would be trench warfare and long periods of continuing strain upon the resources of the combatants. The war, instead of being a hand-to-hand contest, in which the combatants measure their physical and moral superiority, became a kind of stalemate. Neither army was willing to commit totally; being in opposition to each other, they threatened the other and sustained stupendous losses, but were never able to deliver the final and decisive attack.

Britain's Army, the 'Old Contemptibles', which had gone out to France at the beginning of August 1914, was virtually destroyed. By the end of the summer of 1914 the embryonic line of trenches was in position from Switzerland to the English Channel. The days of the dashing mounted officer, in charge of teams of horses limbered up to guns, were just about over when Noel Macklin arrived in France.

On 23 August the Germans came up against the British, who had taken up their position with four divisions on the left of the French at Mons. The power of the defence was shown when the British managed to hold up a force six times their number. Pre-war musketry training paid off, since the most skilled private was able to fire twenty rounds a minute. The Germans believed that each British battalion was equipped with many machine guns, whereas they only had two.

As a lieutenant, Noel Macklin arrived in France about the time of the conclusion of the first battle at Ypres. He was with the 8th Division which included the 5th Brigade of the Royal Horse Artillery and Z Battery, with whom he was serving. When the division moved into the line, it was snowing and bitterly cold.

On 23 November 1914 he was injured at La Basse, close to Givenchy. A high-explosive shell went off very close to him and he was concussed. He was shipped back to England on 26 November. After convalescence he worked in the War Office in London and was sent out to Cairo on a training mission for the Indian Army, who were sending increasingly large numbers of troops to France. He was again examined for health reasons, it was again said he was suffering from concussion and nervous shock as evidenced by sleeplessness, giddiness, loss of memory and mental depression. He resigned his commission and was invalided out in 1915 as a lieutenant, though he had been an acting captain.

Noel Macklin at the wheel of the 100hp Darracq.

He was horrified by the brutality of the war and the unending carnage of horses. There is a story that he lay for hours in a water-sodden shell hole during a bombardment, with his only companion a dead horse; this story is a common one from the sodden fields of Flanders, but may be true in Macklin's case. It may have been the physical and mental stress of forcing horses into trench warfare that contributed to his discharge from the Army. One diagnosis listed by the Army refers to the fact that he was suffering from rheumatism, which would nowadays be diagnosed as arthritis. The arthritis which he suffered for the rest of his life, and which spread over all the joints in his body, was probably initiated by the ice hockey injury and spread by this wartime injury. After convalescence he joined the RNVR in 1916 as a lieutenant and was shore-based on the South Coast for the rest of the war, serving in the Dover Straits Patrol organisation. In 1917 his captaincy was restored to him by the Royal Horse Artillery in his retirement.

Esmé Macklin was divorced from Noel in 1917 and she married Hugh Orr-Ewing in 1922. Noel married Lesley Cordery, whose father was English and mother French, from Picardy. They lived in Glengariff on the Wisley road out of Cobham. Lesley had three sisters – Violette (who later married Lagonda driver/test pilot, John Hindmarsh), Evelyn, and Marese. Noel and Lesley had a son, Lance, born in 1919, who later became a significant name in post-1945 motor racing, and two daughters – Nada and Mia. He also had one daughter out of marriage.

When the USA joined the Allies in 1917, the outcome of the war was in no doubt. Noel and Hugh Orr-Ewing, both having been invalided out of the Army, would have discussed what they were going to do in the post-war scene, and the manufacture of cars was one attractive proposition. Major C.M. Harvey of the Royal Field Artillery, which looked after the heavy guns, would have known Noel during the war, because he was soon driving Eric Campbells in competition after the war.

Noel became interested in ballooning, and especially in the single-seater variant called the 'jump balloons', which allowed a person to jump over obstacles as large as a house. The 'jump balloon' was basically a small balloon of 10–20ft in diameter, with lift provided by coal gas. Sand was carried, to be slowly dumped when the balloon had got to altitude. A saddle was slung from the balloon with no basket to absorb impact damage. Noel never took out a balloon licence from the Royal Aero Club, which may be because he foresaw the dangers of banging into chimney stacks with his left knee – a broken patella is always likely to cause trouble if over-stressed. Noel approached the *Daily Express* to see if he could publicise The International Womans Exhibition by

The jump balloon is launched to demonstrate to
the *Daily Express* the size of the balloon. It had
been suggested a full size balloon could cause
damage to property. The dressed-up jump balloon is
launched with the skirt gathered up and the balloon
then passes over London Docks with skirts down
and the aeronaut peering through a slit in the skirt.

Left: Hugh Orr–Ewing and his wife, previously Esmé Macklin, after the war.

Below: Kathleen Sprake with Noel and their daughter Bunty.

Noel and his wife, Lesley, attend an Etonian function.

over-flying the Olympia Exhibition Hall in London with his balloon dressed up as a woman. First held in 1921, this was a seventeen-day event. This was held again in July 1922 and the *Daily Express* agreed to his proposal. The launch had to be in very still weather with practically no wind, but upwind of Olympia. It is assumed that they loaded the balloon onto an open lorry and coal gas charged it from a convenient gas works. The balloon on the lorry was held down with restraining cables to prevent it becoming airborne until properly positioned. On the third attempt it overflew Olympia very slowly with the intrepid pilot – not Macklin – looking through a slit in the suspended skirt of the woman. On the second attempt it flew along Oxford Street and came down there! Macklin was able to get the agreed cheque for £4,000 from the *Daily Express* for satisfactory promotion of the event.

Macklin always had separate interests, which he would run side-by-side with his money-making projects. His character was not of the 'things will get better' frame of mind, for he was always considering other courses of action and the economic possibilities that other business opportunities could provide. By the early 1920s, 16mm cine film had become available on 50ft spools and film projectors were available to show off amateur films. Professional soundtrack film was also available. He made a soundtrack film – *Noel Duval* – in 1933 when the Invicta sheds were empty of cars. The film centres round the robbery of a pearl necklace from the hero's home; the script is over-complicated, with smugglers, police, a kidnap and a dance, but the Cordery girls who starred were all brilliantly good-looking. Macklin himself was the leading light. The only professional was a girl imported to play the part of the hero's wife, the leading lady. Lesley, Macklin's wife, was cast as the leading lady's mother. Most of the film was shot in the sheds which were the assembly areas for the Invicta and Railton cars, and a number of mounted African animal heads were taken from the house and mounted on the walls to provide an air of verisimilitude.

TWO

MONTE CARLO

Lance Macklin was born in September 1919 and was Noel Macklin's only son; he decided in 1983 that he would collate the papers of his father and family in order to write a family history. Lance wrote:

> What an amazingly versatile mind Noel possessed, and to what lengths he was prepared to go in order to prove, if only to himself, some theory he had in mind. When I was in my twenties discussing Monte Carlo with my Father, he said to me: "'The Law of Chance" is rather like "Perpetual Motion", a lot of brilliant minds have been occupied trying to find solutions to both. One such concerned "The Law of Chance and Probability".'

As far back as 1904 people were publishing papers, articles and books on the various methods and systems for playing the roulette wheel. Even before the turn of the century play had been scientifically studied by mathematicians (or statisticians, as they would be called today). A number of people had successes and the various casinos were not averse to these being publicised to attract more 'plungers', as punters were then known. In 1891 Charles Deville Wells won ¼ million francs at one sitting and broke the tables twelve times in a day. Besides roulette there were always card games, dice and variants such as 'Trente et Quarante', using six packs of cards shuffled together. It was roulette that attracted the publishers of pamphlets offering tips on 'how to win', and these were on sale at every bookstall in France prior to the First World War.

The consensus today is that it is impossible to win roulette by using a system, although the systematic approach has been applied successfully to various card games. However, if a gambler is lucky at roulette and on that day the gods are with him, he will be 'in the vein' and win. Noel Macklin assured the directors of the casino that he was not going to publish his system, but that he was developing it solely for his own benefit. After Lance had interpreted his father's views, most of the family papers were destroyed inadvertently in Spain. The story of how Noel Macklin set out to beat the bank, or just test his system, at Monte Carlo is repeated here, as recorded by Lance Macklin:

After the 1914–18 War Noel left the RNVR and went on holiday to Monte Carlo to rest and recuperate with the family. Was the law of chance unpredictable? He decided to make use of the roulette wheel where there are thirty-six numbers equally divided into red and black segments, and added to this is the number zero which does not have any colour. If one ignores zero, and if the law of chance was precise not only would an exactly equal number of red or black colours come up, but they should alternate in the sequence red – black – red – black – red – black and so on *ad infinitum*. This does not happen in practice and the colours come up in a series of unpredictable sequences.

'Unpredictable' – was it really unpredictable? Noel had spent some holidays in Monte Carlo before the war and, although he was not in the strict sense a gambler, he was, like many other people before him, fascinated by the idea of finding a system which could beat the casino. He purchased various books on the subject and studied all the methods carefully, but soon came to the conclusion that, although some advantage might be gained temporarily by one or two of them, in the long run the casino would always win. Noel purchased the previous hundred issues of a small pamphlet published weekly by the casino which listed in chronological order every single throw which took place at one particular table, from the time it opened for play in the morning, until it closed at night. These hundred pamphlets therefore represented a complete record of the pattern of play at this table over the past two years, and once back in England Noel employed a friend of his who was a retired bank clerk to transcribe all these numbers, as well as the various combinations, such as red and black, odd and even, 1st–2nd–3rd dozen etc. on to graph paper, so that when they were all spread out around the walls of a room, the various lines formed waves of different frequencies and shapes which eventually merged into an even larger overall pattern which could be interpreted to be repetitive.

From this overall picture Noel concluded that, in theory, it should be possible to predict with a certain amount of accuracy (providing the graph was kept up to date) when some of the more unusual phenomena, such as very long runs of red or black etc. were due. The player would be given instruction to wait until red had come up five times and then to place a bet on 'red'. To most people playing at the table this would appear unusual, to say the least, but if red kept coming up the bet was to be left to double up until a run of, say, twelve red had been reached, and only then would it be removed. It was certainly a bold and very original idea but one which Noel decided had to be proved in practice. Accordingly, once the Silver Hawk business closed down, and while various alterations were being carried out on the new house on the Fairmile, he rented a very beautiful villa at Menton, near Monte Carlo, and moved there for six months with the whole family and a number of friends, making the trip by the Blue Train. On their arrival a suite of rooms, taking one whole floor of the Hotel de Paris in Monte Carlo, was taken, and immediately converted into an operations room. The long rows of graphs were set up round the walls, two telephones were installed, and teams of people were formed, comprising some friends, some members of the family, and about three local people, whose jobs included manning the telephones (one line direct to the casino was kept open during the hours of 'play') and updating the graphs every few minutes; one 'professional player' was given written instructions as to what bets to place, what 'runs' they were expecting etc. These professional players were relieved by another one every three hours. Noel himself was usually occupied in the operations room, but one older and trustworthy member of the family was in attendance at the casino at all times.

After a couple of months the system had settled down to normal routine and, although the idea had never been to try and make a lot of money, the results had been consistent and the financial gain sufficient to cover all expenses and maintain the whole family. One day when Noel Macklin was at the casino the director came up to him and said: 'Mr Macklin, I wonder if you would be good enough to explain exactly what it is that you are doing; you see we know from experience the various systems that are available, and normally we can soon deduce which one it is that somebody is using, but with you and your players, while we know that you are winning we are unable to recognise your system.' Noel was amused by this; he explained to the director that it was rather too complicated to understand from a brief description, but that if he would care to drive over to the Hotel de Paris the following morning, Noel would be pleased to show him what they were up to.

The director accepted the invitation. When he arrived he was shown into the operations room by Noel Macklin. According to the family he was completely taken aback; he looked with astonishment at the rows and rows of graphs covering practically the whole wall surface, the different coloured lines indicating various combinations, small flags on pins denoting other points of interest, one attractive girl who seemed to be almost permanently on the telephone, and another one who was busy with a ruler and different coloured crayons and seemed to be engaged in extending the various graphs. Noel quickly explained how it all worked and how much research had had to go into the system for it to have a chance of succeeding. The director, with his years of experience behind him, very quickly absorbed the whole thing, and a worried look came over him. 'Mr Macklin,' he said, 'first of all I would like to thank you for showing me all this and I have to say that I am very impressed. We know at the casino that you have been making money consistently since you have been playing, but as the amounts involved are not, from our point of view, very large and are spread out, we are not worried about that. However, now that you have been good enough to show me your method there is one thing that does worry me.' Noel could not help a slight smile — if nothing else, this was some recognition for his scheme, with the director of the most famous casino in the world admitting that he was worried by it. 'What is it that's worrying you?' Noel asked. The director thought for a moment and then said: 'Mr Macklin, would you mind telling me exactly what your intentions are with regard to your system, I mean, how do you intend to exploit it in the future?' Noel raised one eyebrow, but before he could answer the director went on: 'I mean are you intending to publish a book showing people how it works?' This time Noel laughed out loud: 'Good heavens no, I am only doing it for my own satisfaction, and in order to find out for myself whether or not my idea would actually work if put into practice. We have rented this floor from the Hotel for six months and by the end of that time I should have reached a fairly conclusive result one way or the other, but have no intention of publishing the system or its results.' The director was obviously quite relieved, thanked Noel profusely, and left.

Noel Macklin and the whole family did in fact live a comfortable existence on the earnings from the casino until the six months were up, and then, rather to the relief of the Monte Carlo Casino, they packed up and returned to England.

Many years later with the advent of computers, and by making use of 'walkie-talkies', various people discovered that, by feeding the information from the little pamphlets, so thoughtfully provided by the casino, into a computer, they could considerably improve their chances of winning. Needless to say the Monte Carlo Casino quickly stopped publication of its pamphlet, and anyone found to be making use of telephones, computers or radios, is now instantly banned by all casinos.

THREE

THE ERIC CAMPBELL
AND THE SILVER HAWK

Noel Macklin had been a motoring enthusiast for a long time. During the First World War, as he recovered from front line injuries along with Hugh Orr-Ewing, they discussed the manufacture and funding of a small-engined car with sporting pretensions. The two enthusiasts had no knowledge of car design or of manufacturing capabilities and neither could be described as an engineer. Noel and Hugh's second Christian names were Eric and Campbell respectively, which neither used, so the concept of the Eric Campbell car was born.

One firm who thought they could beat Henry Ford at his own game of a moving-belt twin-track assembly plant was Bean, based in the 'Black Country', Birmingham. In November 1919, Harper Bean Ltd was formed, which brought together Vulcan Motor, Swift of Coventry, Bean Cars, Hadfields (the large Sheffield engineering and steel company), and many component suppliers of radiators, pressings, and steering gear. The intention was to create the General Motors concept within British industry. The stock exchange flotation of Harper Bean Ltd in March of 1919 was a £6 million success, though quite a measurable percentage of the monies promised failed to materialise.

A key figure on the board of directors was Hadfield's Major A.B.H. Clerke. Basil Clerke had been a major in the Royal Artillery serving in India and, when he retired in 1913, he became a director of Hadfields. Hugh Orr-Ewing spent part of his pre-war Army life with the Black Watch in India on the Viceroy General's staff. Noel Macklin had joined the Royal Artillery in 1914 after serving his military apprenticeship and, consequently, both of the Eric Campbell founders could have met and talked about motor cars with Basil Clerke. His Christian name, Augustus, was used for legal documents and the like but he was generally known as Basil. Another gunner whom the founders of Eric Campbell may have met in the pre-war days was Major C.M. Harvey.

Swift had been manufacturers of light motor cars since the turn of the century and had enjoyed limited success with their 7hp cyclecar with a twin-cylinder engine from 1907 to 1913, after which they introduced their 10hp light car. This had a four-cylinder water-cooled engine of 63mm x 90mm which was designed and produced by Swift. It was of impeccable Edwardian engineering provenance with a non-detachable head, external oil pump and long pistons. It was the ED engine of 1,122cc which remained in production from 1914 until 1922. The chassis, though very light, was advanced for its day but without front wheel brakes. The car was announced in the autumn of 1914 when there was a widespread belief that the war would be over by Christmas and it was to be 'business as usual'. Swift undoubtedly piled up a number of chassis which were unsold as the war took its hold. Swift made a number of engineering changes to the car in order for it to be ready for the expected post-war boom, but these 1914 cars were surplus to requirements.

Beans were planning to produce thousands of cars a year using a tracked conveyer system, but their problem was going to be car body construction and the space that this would require.

Handley Page, at the end of the war, had a giant factory in North London, and the Cricklewood Somerton Road works were contracted by Harper Bean to make bodywork for the 11.9 Bean car and to fit this bodywork to the Bean chassis driven over from Tipton. Bean had originally, in 1918, put forward the same deal to Claude Graham-White of the aviation firm Graham White, and the first 2,000 Bean bodies had been made at their Hendon works. Bean placed a second order for a further 5,000. The Graham White company requested an up-front part payment, which was rejected by Bean, who then approached Handley Page.

Frederick Handley Page believed that the contract involving thousands of cars would be worth £750,000. He was to be sorely disappointed. Clerke at this time in 1919 put forward a proposition to manufacture the Eric Campbell to Macklin and Orr-Ewing by taking the redundant chassis of the 1,000cc pre-war Swift, fitting the Coventry-Simplex engine of 66mm x 110 mm (giving a capacity of 1,505cc), and a gearbox. The axle was stated to have a high axle ratio.

To get the project started, the first batch of chassis were fitted with Swift engines. Two radiator manufacturers were part of the Bean empire and the radiator could be produced in-house. A further embellishment aimed at creating a sporty appearance was the fitting of wire wheels instead of the more plebeian artillery wheels. Extra chassis bracing for the sports car image was agreed, plus fitting a two-seater body. All the final assembly was to be carried out at Handley Page.

Handley Page, having agreed the specification with Bean, who acted as agent, would have no dealings with Macklin and Orr-Ewing, and there would be no possibility of them interfering on any basis with the design or manufacture. Their responsibility, as Handley Page saw it, was for Eric Campbell, a sub-contractor to Bean, to take the completed cars from Cricklewood and market them. Clerke made the introduction to Frederick Handley Page, who it can be inferred, rejected a limited production run, but stated that the new car could be a sub-contract within the Bean commitment.

Noel Macklin appreciated that he needed staff and especially staff who were well briefed on automotive matters and had knowledge of the industry. He placed a free advertisement in the *Daily Mail* in 1920. There was widespread unemployment at the time and the *Daily Mail* served a useful purpose in offering this service to people. William Watson, then twenty-seven years of age, had been apprenticed in an ironworks, served in the Royal Naval Air Service during the war and was at the time working for Bayliss Thomas. He only worked at Eric Campbell for a week or so, while on holiday, but he enjoyed the company. He impressed Noel Macklin.

The Eric Campbell car took shape and the contract for manufacture was probably a gentleman's agreement negotiated direct with Hadfields, who took it upon themselves to be the suppliers to Messrs Macklin and Orr-Ewing, with the final assembly and bodywork on the Swift chassis being carried out by Handley Page. The car was to be promoted as 'The Yacht of the Road'. How many were made it is impossible to determine but it is probable that the first batch would be envisaged as numbering about 100 cars. It is extremely likely that around fifty cars were delivered to Macklin, and the later production of simplified and cheaper Eric Campbells by Vulcan, with an infusion of other redundant Swift chassis, was a move later instigated by Hadfields to get some money back.

Noel was quite sure that a pretty woman could sell anything and he recruited Kathleen Sprake to be a driver in rallies and trials with an Eric Campbell. He installed her in Aldingbourne House, Chichester. The house was the birthplace of Richard Seaman. She became pregnant by Noel and changed her name by deed poll so that her child would be a Macklin. Noel's daughter, Bunty, was born within a few days of the birth of his son, Lance Macklin. There was a popular song of the time called 'Bunty'. Kathleen did not use the surname Macklin except when dealing with legal matters, and she stayed, for all other purposes, a Sprake.

Handley Page fell out with Harper Bean on unpaid accounts. The Eric Campbell account which was a sub-contract through Harper Bean became lost in the arguments following the bankruptcy of the Harper Bean conglomerate at the

The first Eric Campbell at the South Harting Speed Trials of 1919 with Noel Macklin at the wheel, captioned by Noel Macklin in Jockey Club terms as at the 'weigh-in'. The resemblance to the Rolls-Royce radiator shape is striking.

Aldingbourne House. An Eric Campbell outside the house where Kathleen Sprake had been installed to give birth to her daughter Bunty.

end of 1920. A. Harper Sons & Bean was soon reconstituted out of the remains of the previous organisation by buying out their part from the conglomerate, but the financial connection with Macklin and Orr-Ewing was in the past.

Noel Macklin insisted throughout his motoring life that cars had to be seen in competition. In July 1919 the Essex Motor Club held a sprint on the western esplanade of Westcliff-on-Sea. A number of Eric Campbells were entered, but were captioned in the programme as Campbells. The drivers were Captains Orr-Ewing and Macklin, W. Barnato and Miss Arnaud. One of the first motor races held after the First World War was the 1919 Targa Florio in November. Two Eric Campbells were entered for Jack Scales and Cyril Snipe, but the Scales car was the only one that ran, and not very satisfactorily. The 1,505cc capacity of the Coventry-Simplex engine was impractical for competition, and the engine was reduced to 1,500cc by restroking to a 109.5mm stroke, giving a capacity of 1,498cc.

Macklin recruited the beautiful Kathleen Sprake to go for long-distance records. Miss Kathleen Sprake set off on a 25,000 mile proving journey through Europe and Africa in an Eric Campbell, and gained a level of publicity due to being a good-looking young woman. She had only got to the north of England when the newsworthiness of such a trip dried up. Miss Violette Cordery, Macklin's sister-in-

The Royal Artillery. Major Harvey, later to be a prominent Alvis man, has Captain Noel Macklin as his navigator.

Above: Noel Macklin on the Portsmouth road close to the 'hut' (an important cyclist venue of the 1890s) in EC2115.

Left: Violette Cordery at the wheel of EC2115. This photograph was most likely taken by Cecil Macklin, who was keen on photography. A number of the early photographs in this book were probably taken by him.

law, was also very good-looking, and won a race for lady drivers at Brooklands in an Eric Campbell in May 1920. About twenty firms had signed up as agents, of which Wood & Lambert of Stamford Hill in London were the most active, taking up to five cars at a time. When the time came to forget about the Eric Campbell, Wood & Lambert took the remaindered cars from Cobham and seriously discounted them to sell them off.

There were too many manufacturers following the same route of assembly of components and marketing them as a car for the Eric Campbell to survive. The Harper Bean operation took over the Eric Campbell, simplifying the design and reducing costs for continued construction. Badge-engineered Eric Campbells made out of redundant design Swifts had an appeal. A number of bodies were fitted, and alternative Swift engines were added. Such luxury fittings as wire wheels were replaced by spoked artillery wheels, and later by pressed-steel wheels, but the new company, the Vulcan Iron & Metal Works (1918), based in Southall, West London, failed to sell the considerably lower priced Eric Campbell, and manufacture ceased by 1926. About a dozen unsold cars from the first batch of Eric Campbells, which Macklin had taken delivery of and presumably paid for, were to become Silver Hawks. The remaining cars of Macklin specification were put on sale by Wood & Lambert, and those of Harper Bean specification by Vulcan.

In 1924 William Watson re-entered the scene at Cobham after being invited to meet the Lyle brothers. He gathered through conversation that Noel and Hugh were both lucky to get out of the Harper Bean deal without having to pay out a large sum of money for cancellation of the contract. Macklin told Watson of his experiments with steam-powered cars and of his intent to build a top-gear car. Watson was told that as soon as arrangements could be made for production in adequate premises that he would be employed there and then.

Kathleen Sprake and an RAC observer at the commencement of the 25,000-mile run.

Probably the first Silver Hawk with Violette Cordery at the wheel. Behind are Messrs Gedge, Bing, Watson and Macklin. Watson was only just in the 5ft-plus height category, and therefore makes Macklin look tall.

Noel Macklin competes in a Silver Hawk.

Probably the last of the small batch of Silver Hawks produced.

Noel had moved house post-war to Glengariff on the Wisley road out of Cobham. In the sheds adjoining his new Cobham home, he evolved the Silver Hawk, intended as a production sports-racing car. This was produced only in chassis form and was based on an uprated and improved Eric Campbell frame, which in its turn was based on a Swift frame, and was powered by a modified Coventry-Simplex engine. At least one car was built with a 1,498cc Sage engine of the L-head type, known nowadays as a side valve, with aluminium pistons and nickel steel connecting rods.

Another engine that was tried was the Italian four-cylinder 1,500cc single ohc FAST, which probably came via George Duller, but, although the Silver Hawk achieved reasonable success at Brooklands in the hands of George Duller and C.M. Harvey (both better known as Alvis drivers), as well as Violet Cordery and Macklin himself, the market for such a car was limited and it was not a commercial success, since they had no manufacturing capability. Noel Macklin still believed in the dictum that the man who built a better mousetrap would have the public beating a path to his door, but he found that that this was not necessarily the case.

Bean had confirmed to their own satisfaction that badge-engineered Swift cars, sold as Eric Campbells, did sell, and they then put together low-cost Eric

Noel Macklin and William Watson in the yard at Glengariff with a Silver Hawk.

The front of Glengariff.

The redundant agricultural/equine sheds at Glengariff were intended to be the centre of operations for building Silver Hawks. This was probably the first Silver Hawk for sale, with Violette Cordery waiting off-stage.

Oliver Lyle visits Glengariff and tries out a Silver Hawk.

The 10–22hp Eric Campbell for the 1922 Motor Show at the White City, as offered by Dobson and Smith Ltd of Knightsbridge (acting as sole concessionaires for the Vulcan Iron & Metal Works of Southall, Middlesex).

Campbells, with luxury items such as wire wheels entirely dispensed with in favour of pressed wheels and obsolete Swift equipment, to be recycled as Eric Campbells and sold by Vulcan.

FOUR

THE INVICTA

Noel Macklin was very astute in the use of money and endeavoured to persuade other people to finance his business operations. He had learnt a considerable number of business truths with the manufacture and selling of the Eric Campbell.

He retained management and ownership of all his enterprises. He wooed friends into investing in his activities. He was also adept in keeping from these investors that there were other investors.

His principal method of influencing decisions was to introduce ideas to other people who tended to repeat them back to him with a variation. Macklin would then say: 'What a good idea – we will carry that through.'

Hugh Orr-Ewing had been the principal subscriber to the Eric Campbell and, seemingly without knowing of the Lyles' financial involvement, carried on investing in the Invicta.

There was not a motoring soul during the First World War who did not believe that there would be a vast post-war market for cars. The pre-war mass production success of Ford with the Model T, both in America and at Trafford Park, Manchester, together with William Morris's Cowley models, was a sign of things to come.

In the first years of peace following the end of the war Captain Noel Macklin did a certain amount of competitive motoring, driving Eric Campbells, and it is probable that his troubled knee caused him further discomfort. Since the injury was in his left leg, his clutch leg, it was almost certainly the cause of his interest in single-gear clutchless motoring, which meant top-gear motoring.

Towards the end of the war in 1917 Noel Macklin, while on convalescent leave from the Army and negotiating to join the RNVR for a shore-based commission,

We confidently offer the **INVICTA** to the public as a successful attempt to effect a radical improvement in motor cars. It combines in a manner achieved by no other car seven qualities which are probably those most sought after by the motorist, namely:—

1. *The flexibility of the good American cars.*
2. *The speed and road-holding of the best European sports cars.*
3. *A delicacy of control not found on any other car.*
4. *An unique top gear performance.*
5. *A long-lasting reliability which has in public competition never been equalled.*
6. *Absolutely certain and instantaneous engine-starting at all temperatures.*
7. *A service and guarantee which are the acme of generosity and despatch.*

The first Invicta sales catalogue with words by Oliver Lyle, and (*right*) the Invicta motif.

bought a 1908 period Stanley Steam car, and in 1918 quickly obtained a post-war example, through the good offices of the Lyle brothers. The Stanley was not without its faults, and the principal one was the lack of instant steam on starting up from scratch. Also, the continued use of a heavy throttle would exhaust boiler pressure. He had renewed acquaintance with the Lyle brothers in 1923, having met them in Monte Carlo in 1920–21. In 1959, Oliver Lyle wrote to Michael Sedgwick when he was researching *Lost Causes of Motoring.* He said: 'Macklin was engaging his untiring energy and ingenuity on something entirely unconnected with motorcars, which looked like petering out.' He wrote further to Michael Sedgwick about his brother Philip Lyle:

> [Philip] had owned many steam cars and both he and I longed for a car like the Stanley, without its serious drawbacks. We agreed that Macklin should study the production of the steam car, so we imported a Doble, the latest and most advanced steam car, and we sent it to Cobham where we had installed Macklin on the Fairmile. For months we worked at the steam car trying to make it practical and simpler – the Doble though beautifully made was very complicated.

The sophisticated Doble came on the market with more or less instant starting from cold, and enough steam pressure to allow for four flat-out laps of Brooklands. The Doble was probably the first car to have an electric management system and this was not altogether fault-free. A persistent defect involved steam generation not shutting down when the car was at rest. Several times the safety valve blew off when the car was parked. The car would release steam, leading bystanders to believe that it was either on fire or about to blow up. Noel Macklin knew that the simple way to deal with this was to accelerate hard down the road to drop the boiler pressure before returning and checking the flame heating was set in a tick-over state. This unfortunate 'blow-up' occurrence happened one day outside the Dorchester Hotel in the West End of London, and again in Richmond High Street. Fire brigades were involved on both occasions. Noel wrote:

> Compared with the power given by petrol engines, the steam car was at an ever-increasing disadvantage – the fundamental reason being the size of fire. A petrol engine burns its fuel under a pressure of about 6 atmospheres, whereas a steam car burns it at 1 atmosphere. So, when the first Invicta, with its Meadows engine, had shown its performance, we decided to produce it and to abandon work on steam cars. The decision was taken to forget about a Doble agency.

Then came the momentous conversion, as recorded by Oliver Lyle: 'my brother's wife said to him: "Phil, I don't believe I shall ever be able to change gear properly." Noel Macklin said: "Eileen, I'll make you a car on which you won't have to change gear."' Thus was the top-gear car initiated (the specification included the ability to start in top gear up a number of steepish ascents such as Guildford High Street).

Oliver Lyle wrote:

> My brother and I financed the Invicta from the start until Lord Fitzwilliam took over, apart from some working capital provided by Carl Miesegaes, who lived close to my brother on the Hogs Back and was a sugar broker. I devoted much more time (and money) to Invicta than my brother and I was much more enthusiastic than Macklin on the top-gear idea. Macklin was a sports car man at heart – he had been taught racing driving by Nazarro. While Macklin produced the Invicta for my sister-in-law, I suppose it could be said that I was the moving spirit in producing it for sale. At that time I was forever saying that I had changed gear one million times and that I thought it was 900,000 times too often.

Macklin required more land to venture into serious car production and, from the Glengariff house on the Wisley road out of Cobham, he moved to the Fairmile, which was on the main London road running out of Cobham. Seeing how little progress had been made in building workshops and equipping them since Macklin had moved in, the Lyle brothers, being the dominant owners of sugar manufacturers

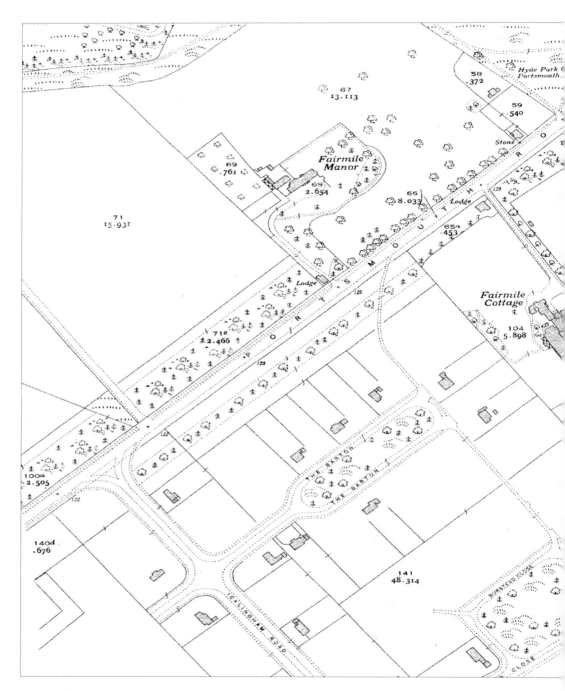

Section of a 1934 local authority drawing of the Fairmile Estate on the Portsmouth road. It shows the Lodge on the main road (still extant) and the house (the Fairmile Cottage) with the outbuildings used for the Invicta and Railton cars.

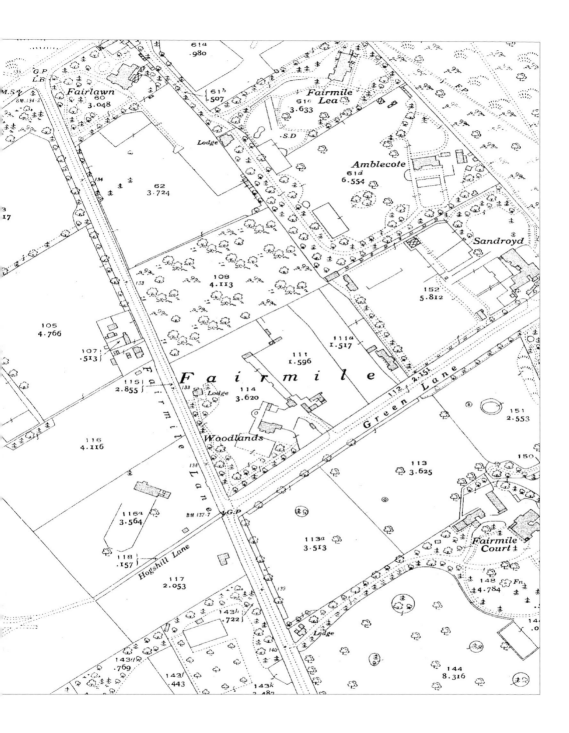

Left: Sir Oliver Lyle. Born 1890, died 1961. In the First World War he served as a captain in the Highland Light Infantry and was wounded. He was subsequently employed by the Inventions Department of the Ministry of Munitions and was made an OBE. In 1919 he became a director of Tate & Lyle and was vice chairman at the time he retired. He was knighted in the Second World War for his work on fuel efficiency. At Tate & Lyle he was known as 'Olly' and was always approachable, kind, considerate and amusing.

Below: An early 2½-litre car with artillery wheels.

Phillip Lyle and his wife Eileen. Eileen was quoted by Noel Macklin as the person responsible for the top-gear performance of the Invicta.

Phillip and Eileen Lyle on holiday in the Alps with their two Invictas, to which they transferred an earlier Surrey registration number.

An economy long-wheelbase 2½-litre Invicta saloon with artillery wheels. This was Cushman's transport, until it was sold.

Tate & Lyle, contacted Higgs & Hill, the favoured building contractor used by the sugar company, asking them to come to the Fairmile. New buildings were built as extensions to the stables, and the property had ample grounds for expansion. A gate house guarded the entrance to the estate off the main road, and the house became Macklin's home from home. The prototypes of the Invicta, as the new make was to be called, were built in the stables and coach house. The word *invicta* means 'unconquered', but tends to be interpreted as 'the conquerer'.

The first person Macklin appointed was William Watson, who came to him from the Bayliss Thomas car operation, part of the then Excelsior Motor Cycle Co. Watson brought with him a number of Bayliss Thomas chassis from Birmingham, which could be modified by taking out the cross-bracing and moving them backward in the chassis to accommodate the specified Macklin engine.

Macklin recognised that he could not depend on sub-contractors to build complete motor cars, though he would very much like to, and so therefore needed staff. He had discussions with many people at this stage and he received a considerable amount of advice from Parry Thomas, who backed his own judgment by becoming an early owner of an Invicta and fitted a 3-litre four-cylinder Italian FAST engine, with which he competed at Brooklands.

After the First World War there came a surge in the introduction of new ideas into automobile engineering. Prior to the war the fixed non-detachable head engine was the norm for production vehicles. After the war, the detachable head, with inlet valves over the exhaust valves in the cylinder block, provided the opportunity for higher compression ratios and a sculpting of the combustion area shape.

The motor industry was, from the mid-1920s to the early 1930s, dominated by the small six, of which the AC Six was probably the best example. The Coventry-Simplex and the Coventry-Climax were built in the same factory. The Simplex engines were classically Edwardian in design with a fixed head and valves held in detachable pockets. The Climax had a detachable head, with separately mounted overheard camshaft to operate the two inlet valves per cylinder, while the exhaust valves were in the block, providing an inlet-over-exhaust combustion area, which meant that various design changes offered up a more compact combustion chamber per cylinder and a higher compression ratio, leading to higher power and better gas flow. The original Macklin Invicta, built in 1924–25, had this new good-looking Coventry-Climax overhead-camshaft six-cylinder 2-litre engine and a three-speed gearbox in a 10ft wheelbase chassis, ex-Bayliss Thomas, with four-seater tourer coachwork. Artillery wheels were fitted to early cars. Transmission to the 4.9-ratio Moss rear axle was via an open propeller shaft with a Rubery Owen front axle and a Marles steering assembly. Alford & Alder brakes on the front axle completed the mechanical melange. The quality image may have been damaged by the use of artillery wheels. This combination of various proprietary components was reasonably successful. The power unit lacked the flexibility, quietness of running and effortless power which the six-cylinder concept promised and which Macklin sought. The engine was later developed to become a smooth-running unit, but this would take several years. Six engines had been bought. The first three engines had been installed in the modified chassis and were ready to be fitted with bodies. They had been assembled in the stables and were standing outside under the glass roof of the stables washing area, when a snap frost caused the engines to ice up. Fortunately the heads were removed the next day when no trouble had arisen.

The social connection between Parry Thomas and Noel Macklin was well-known, and Parry Thomas used to call in at the Fairmile, but there was undoubtedly a professional element to the friendship.

A chance meeting with a director of Henry Meadows Ltd of Wolverhampton led to an agreement whereby Macklin was to be supplied with the 2,692cc Meadows six-cylinder ohv engine and four-speed gearbox. This was the first time that the Beverley Barnes organisation came into the Invicta equation, by building a rear axle to join up with the Meadows four-speed gearbox via a

The 3-litre engine with twin Solexes.

universal jointed propeller shaft. In this form the Invicta entered production and road tests revealed that most of Macklin's aims had been fulfilled. The Invicta would accelerate in top gear from 10 to 60mph in an effortless twenty-seven seconds, and could climb the very steep Brooklands test hill, which at its steepest point had a gradient of 1:4, on the same ratio. This was at the expense of top speed, which was just over 60mph. This top speed was perfectly satisfactory for the single-speed type of motorist, but it was not sporting — 65–70 mph would have been the requirements of the time. The Meadows engine built at Fallings Park, Wolverhampton, was adopted in 2.5 litre form but before the first chassis were delivered to the coach builder, the order was changed to the modified 3 litre truck engine developed by Henry Meadows. This had a higher revolution range, suitable for cars. Gear ratios were 13:1, 8:1, 6.1:1 and 4.5:1. The specification provided 55–60bhp at 3,000rpm, on a 9ft 4in wheelbase, weighing approximately 1 ton with front wheel brakes. A thermostat and water pump were fitted, but no fan. There were two and a half turns lock-to-lock of the Marles steering, which was high gearing for a large car. The suspension consisted of elliptic leaf springs, with the after ones free to slide at one end in bronze bearings. This sliding end was a feature of all Invictas as it was believed to help to reduce 'bump' steer.

Oliver Lyle disliked the style and content of the owner handbooks issued by competitors, and so he wrote the first Invicta handbook himself. Oliver Lyle's input in the marketing of the Invicta was very important to the company. Sales were to be handled by George England Ltd, South Molton Street, London. Maximum speed with the 3 litre version of the Meadows engine was now 70mph, and in this form it was a fine sporting car and an extremely attractive touring car. Noel Macklin, Watson and Parry Thomas recognised the strength and size of the Meadows company and Noel Macklin went out of his way to cultivate a close relationship with Henry Meadows himself, as well as with Crump, the engine designer. Years later Crump told this author that they made modifications to suit Invicta and that these always cost money, which they found difficult to recover – so much so that the company evolved the ethos that they only sold standard engines, unless they had an order to specifically carry through some modification. This concept of rigorous financial containment was also applied to Lea-Francis and AFN Ltd with Frazer Nash 1,500cc 4ED engines.

The Invicta with the 3-litre engine ascended Brooklands test hill in top gear, with a good performance from 10mph in top gear. Rudge Whitworth hubs of 52mm, with splined wheels and knock-off hub nuts, were soon incorporated to complete the sports car specification. The pricing was £595 for the short chassis and £610 for the long chassis. Bodies were built by coach builders and were an extra price.

The Bayliss Thomas chassis had a tendency to sag with the extra weight and William Watson designed the LC (Large Chassis) frame, which was manufactured by Thompsons of Bilston, Staffordshire. This was likely to have been a variant of other chassis frames made by that company.

In July 1925 came the occasion of the first competitive entries for the West Kent Brooklands meeting. In the ½ mile scratch race, Miss Violette Cordery came first, Oliver Lyle second, and 'the remainder of the field hardly got going'. Tapleys presented a gradient meter to anyone whose car could climb a 1:7 hill in top gear. Invicta won the prize.

Noel Macklin, with Watson, had recruited staff for the manufacture of the Invicta and a number of his employees were ex-GN mechanics from the collapsed GN cyclecar firm. One of the ex-GN mechanics employed by Invicta told Violette Cordery that 'Cushie' Cushman had left Archie Frazer-Nash's employ at Frazer Nash Ltd, as that company had amalgamated with William G. Thomas Ltd on the opposite side of London Road in Kingston-upon-Thames.

Left and below: William Watson gets married in 1925. He was lent one of the new 3-litre models for his honeymoon.

Thomas had a works manager and there was no room for Cushman. Violette Cordery immediately employed Cushman to come to Monza as the chef d'equipe for the Invicta attack on world records.

There were two L.A. Cushmans active in motor racing in the early 1920s. The other Cushman was a Frenchman who drove many different cars, but primarily Bugattis. 'Cushie' had for years been the principal mechanic and manager for the GN competitions department. His principal duty was to Archie Nash in the preparation and racing of GNs. Archie Nash, trading as Frazer Nash by 1923, took 'Cushie' to Kingston-upon-Thames for the beginnings of Frazer Nash Ltd.

GN Ltd had advertised wisely, but their chief promotional weapon had been motoring competition. Noel Macklin did not need any prompting to follow the same path as GN, for with the plethora of manufacturers and assemblers offering cars in 1924, the only real alternative method of promotion was the ever lowering price systems adopted by Morris, Bean and Austin.

A long-distance record at Monza was the aim in a 3-litre driven by Violette Cordery with two male backup drivers. The 1920s was an era of record breaking

A fabric-bodied 2½-litre Invicta at Cushman's home in East Horsley, Surrey.

A short-wheelbase 3-litre Invicta bodied by Newns, a much favoured coachwork firm through the Invicta and Railton days. Note the Invicta motif on the radiator cap – a very rare fitting.

Cushman sits proudly in the Invicta prior to the start of the Monza record attempt.

The Monza team. Toby Howard, Edward Mills, Violette Cordery, 'Cushie' Cushman, and Moy.

and Macklin was anxious to gain publicity in this field, since bonuses were paid by the tyre, oil and accessory firms for national and international records. With Miss Violette Cordery as driver, a sister of Macklin's second wife and also good-looking, the first attempt was to cover 25,000 miles of continuous running at Monza, at an average of no less than 50mph. The male team that went out were Cushman, Howard Mills, Garland, Moy, and Brown. All went well until, at 5,000 miles, one of the male drivers was involved in a violent collision with the iron railings lining the course after he had fallen asleep at the wheel. The car was repaired in the Isotta Fraschini works, Milan, but was subsequently delayed by fracture of the chassis on the rough course. At 20,000 miles the first attempt was abandoned. They had taken another Invicta out to Monza to use as hack transport and, using this car's chassis, and the engine, transmission, and strapped-together bodywork from the first car, a second attempt was made. The light touring body fitted made by Compton & Hermon of Walton-on-Thames, was transferred, as was the engine and back axle, to the new chassis in the Isotta Fraschini factory in Milan. Compton & Hermon had taken a licence from Gordon England to use this lightweight racing design utilising plywood panels and box girders with a fabric skin over the whole.

Four international and thirty-three Italian national records were broken. The records established were 10,000 miles at 56.47mph and 15,000 miles at 55.76mph. The car was exhibited at Selfridges in London on completion of the run. On his return from Monza, Macklin hired Cushman, in recognition of his sterling work in Italy as works manager for Invicta. Noel Macklin also gave a silver cup commemorating the event to each and every member of the team.

Later, in July 1926, Miss Cordery gained a certificate from the RAC for covering 5,000 miles, the car was fitted with twin Solex carburettors. The car was driven by Violette Cordery, where she achieved 3,000, 4,000, 5,000 miles, and 4,000 and 5,000km at over 70mph. The 3-litre Meadows with a 3.6:1 top gear had a weight of 19¾ hundredweights. The first attempt at Brooklands, running only in the daylight hours, had failed with universal-joint trouble. On the second attempt 5,016.2 miles was covered at average speeds of 70.7mph, including stops (stops and repairs occupied two hours forty-five minutes). The water pump gland was tightened seven times, a new water pump fitted, the carburettor jets changed, the magneto contact breaker adjusted, a new contact breaker fitted, the shock absorbers adjusted and a bolt replaced, the radiator repaired, the vacuum tank cleaned, and a new engine holding-down bolt fitted. Also in July 1926 the same car and driver at Montlhery in France ran 5,000 miles in seventy-one hours, averaging 70.7mph and taking five more world records under RAC observation. The Dewar Trophy was won.

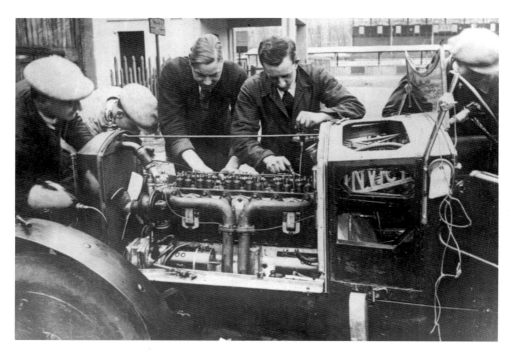

The car is prepared for the Monthlery record attempt. Note the Invicta aluminium casting supporting the instrument panel.

After the crash at Monza the car was repaired in Isotta Fraschini's factory in Milan. The car is fitted with an extra leather belt to fasten the body to the chassis and new tyres. The steering is being adjusted, prior to starting the record attempt all over again.

The car is rebuilt after the return from Monza in preparation for the record attempts at Monthlery, near Paris.

Success at Monza

August 1929 – an observed record. Violette Cordery with her eighteen-year-old younger sister, Evelyn, perched behind her. They had both run in three hour sessions at Brooklands for forty-five days. Excluding Sundays, they started at 8 a.m. and went for twelve hours per day until they recorded 30,000 miles in 30,000 minutes (10,000 laps of Brooklands). Two of the three children at the rear of the car are Macklin's daughters, and behind them stands Noel's wife wearing her pearls.

It was recorded at the time by Douglas Irvine in an interview with a mechanic:

Never were there such perfect working conditions or such a delightful 'Boss' to work for, as Captain Noel Macklin, who became affectionately known to his workforce as 'The Prince', because of his charm and superb tact in handling labour. The workforce in those days, which started with four men, and reached twenty-eight hands, was led by Ernest Hatcher, who was previously a racing mechanic to Scriven, the Austin 20 racing driver. He was later joined by Arthur Shadwick from Frazer Nash and Arthur Roberts, who later worked on the Napier-Railton, in preparation for John Cobb's land-speed-record attempt, was another recruit. It was a happy works, with all the rest of them – Bill Stringer and Ted Riggs, the mechanics; Tubbs the chargehand; Bill Mills; Bill Smith; Rawlings; and the two Barrett brothers, 'Holly' Bright, who later set up his own establishment preparing racing cars for international events. All under the fatherly eye of Cushie Cushman, the Works Manager, also late of Frazer Nash. At Invicta all of us had GNs. Cushman and Shadwick had really super ohv ones. Cushman was very kind. Whenever we needed a spare part he would bring us one from his own collection and charge us only half-a-crown for it.

The 3-litre Invicta on the Round-the-World Tour.

Later, the first brochure was produced and Oliver Lyle insisted that he should write it and that the usual hyperbole of automotive writers in promoting a product was to be avoided.

Macklin was concerned that the costings of assembling a car for which he only had to make very few parts seemed to be out of control. The other aspect that was causing problems was the lack of space for assembly. A lot of space was taken up by the servicing of client's cars. Macklin had found himself from the start in the role of works manager and his softly-worded, considerate manner was not ideal for this role. After Cushman was established, he and Watson agreed that the space at the Fairmile was inadequate for the construction of cars, even though all the components were bought in and the coachbuilding was done elsewhere. It was put to Macklin that the space would be adequate for the production of twenty to forty cars a year if the assembly of the chassis was done elsewhere and the only scheduled work at the Fairmile was electrification, finishing off, road-testing, checking out finished cars, and servicing. This would be an ideal solution to the space problem. Macklin was not averse to the suggestions, as he had found that the cost of work done at Cobham was high. Messrs Lenaerts (a count) and

Mr Hatcher, the mechanic, shows off the two Solex carburettors to Violette Cordery

Dolphens, at Beverley Barnes in Barnes, west London, quoted for the assembly of the cars, and their quote was accepted. Beverley Barnes was a Belgian-owned business, and Bentley of Cricklewood, who also had space problems, was a major client. This meant that Invicta components, such as engines, could be delivered by the manufacturers direct to Barnes. Shortly after finalising the build with Beverley Barnes the contract was extended to wiring up and electrical installation of lights to be carried out by Invicta staff at Barnes. Final road-testing involved a 1,000-mile running-in procedure, with testing on known steep hills in top gear carried out from the Fairmile base.

The successes of 1926 were surpassed in 1927, when the same driver and car won a second Dewar Trophy with a world tour covering some 10,000 miles. Violette Cordery's world tour in PF 6849 involved a crew comprising Ernest Hatcher – always referred to as 'Mr Hatcher the mechanic' – with Miss Simpson, a trained nurse, and Mr Spragge, an RAC observer. A collapsible tent was rolled up on the near side of the body.

An *Autocar* editorial hailed this as a good advertisement for the British motor industry. The start was on 9 February 1927 and the route was planned via

In North Africa, having a picnic lunch with the nurse.

A 3-litre Invicta with what looks like a Newns body.

France, Algeria, India, Australia, USA and Canada. The car was in India in April. The finish was at Hyde Park Hotel in July. The major upset on the trip was an incident in which the car was damaged by a runaway tram in Africa.

The successful team was welcomed on return to London by Lord Dewar and Sir Charles Wakefield. The road mileage was 10,266 in total. Rear axle shafts and bearings had been renewed, as had all four rear brake shoes. Twenty-four covers and tubes were used. The average speed over the 10,000 miles was 24.6mph when underway.

The Monza Run had established the Invicta as a performance car with excellent reliability – the round-the-world tour had proved the car's impressive reliability by the standards of the time – but it was not yet a *high* performance car. This aspect was eventually highlighted in 1928 when, at the Olympia Show, Invicta unveiled its latest model with a 4½-litre Meadows engine, rated at 30hp (RAC). Here, at last, was an Invicta with real performance and, for the late 1920s, quite shattering acceleration, yet still retaining the top-gear flexibility that was Macklin's ideal.

Considerable changes were made to the range when a twin-plug cylinder head was introduced for the 3-litre model and dual ignition with magneto and coil provided. At the Motor Show the new 4½-litre model was added to the range. Watson had developed a modified cylinder head with larger valves and better ports but, when fitted to the 3-litre engine, this was not a success. With the 4½-litre engine, it was absolutely perfect. It was claimed that the new engine developed 110bhp at 3,200rpm, but this appears to be optimistic as, when the same engine was first used by Lagonda in 1933, the makers claimed an output of 103bhp. Even so, the existing 3-litre chassis was far too light and flexible for the increased power. Two chassis lengths, the LC (10ft wheelbase) and the SC (9ft wheelbase) were now available. In 1929 a completely redesigned chassis, with heavier and deeper side-members, stiffer cross-bracing, lowered radiator line and an increased track of 4ft 8in, was introduced. Wheelbase was standardised at 10ft 6in and shortly afterwards at 10ft and, in the interests of economy, the last of the 3-litre cars used this chassis. The chassis was priced at £1,050, which approximated closely to the price of Bentley and Rolls-Royce. To overcome engine failure, heavier section duralumin connecting rods were henceforth fitted and 'electron' gearbox and crankcase castings were introduced.

Macklin had slowly been letting the fitters go, as Beverley Barnes took over the responsibility of production. It was 'Cushie' Cushman who was the contact that made it all work. Noel Macklin had made a lot of contacts through the Brooklands circuit and, since he was quiet and self-contained, the design connections he built up, primarily through Reid Railton and Thompson and Taylor, were not widely known.

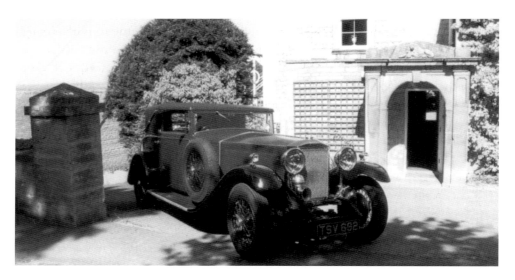

A high-chassis 4½-litre.

In 1929 another long-distance run was mounted at Brooklands using the daylight hours only, and a distance of 30,000 miles was covered in 30,000 minutes.

Shortly after the 1929 announcement of all the design improvements, and the release of William Watson on to the labour market, came the savage price cutting. This policy caused considerable disagreement within the management of the company, as a number of drastic changes in the specification were made. The 4½, chassis only, was dropped from £1,050 to £650, and the 3-litre model was dropped from the range altogether. One of the disturbing economies to potential clients was to fit smaller Smiths instruments to the dashboard. The guarantee, which had previously included labour, was reduced from three years to six months, a plated brass radiator replaced the former nickel silver one, cheaper steel castings were used for certain chassis components and inferior electrics were fitted. Nevertheless, despite these changes and after heavy discussions with Beverley Barnes about streamlined production methods, the basic build quality of the chassis was unchanged, and so production of the cheap Invicta was not economically viable following the price cuts.

It can be deduced, with hindsight, that at this moment Noel Macklin lost faith in Invicta and realised that, in competition with many other British firms, such as Lagonda, Talbot, Sunbeam, Bentley and others, let alone the Continental manufacturers, such as Bugatti and Alfa Romeo, he was going to be hard-pressed to survive. Competition was intense for cars that represented excellence, performance and quality.

The first important example of Reid Railton's involvement with Invicta is the 1931 single-seater Invicta, which was built for Dudley Froy to drive in the 500 Mile Race. The build was slow in maturing as it involved a number of engineering changes to the standard chassis, such as moving the engine backwards. The Fairmile facilities were therefore insufficient. It was therefore necessary for the work to be done elsewhere, probably by Thomson and Taylor direct. Macklin was reluctant to find the money, and Froy refused to fund the project. The car was completed in time for the 1932 500 Mile Race but crashed in practice and was never resuscitated.

This was an exceedingly difficult period for all branches of the motor industry, and the most outstanding Invicta model, the S-Type, more familiarly known as the '100mph' model, was not a commercial success, with only sixty-seven being built. Despite the '100mph' title given to the model, true top speed was a little over 90mph under favourable conditions, but it would pull as low as 6mph in top gear without snatch. The S-Type had a nickel chrome steel frame swept over the front axle and underslung at the rear, with flattened rear springs outside the frame. A close ratio gearbox and a higher ratio 3.6:1 rear axle were used. The appearance was particularly attractive – a chromium-plated nickel-steel radiator, flexible external exhausts and a slab fuel tank mounted at the rear of the low-slung tourer

An S-Type four-seater coachwork by Carbodies.

The 4½-litre Meadows engine as shown in the Invicta catalogue.

coachwork all contributed to a handsome sporting appearance. The S-Type was priced at £750 in chassis form or £950 with 2/4-seater tourer coachwork.

Unfortunately the model gained a reputation for unstable roadholding, which stemmed from an accident involving Sammy Davis when he was driving one of the cars at Brooklands in 1931. However, apart from this, there are few recorded accidents involving Invictas. It is nonetheless true that a low-built car, with non-independent front suspension and a greater proportion of weight on the front wheels than on the rear wheels, with little weight in the centre section, will have a chassis that is inclined to sudden breakaway at the rear in wet conditions. Add to this a predisposition to understeer and the fact that the tyres of the period and, indeed, up to the advent of the Michelin X in the post-war years, had rigid side walls and non-flexible covers, and it is little surprise that, when an S-Type was lent to Humphrey Cook, the man behind the ERA, for him to drive around central London (Noel Macklin was endeavouring to gain financial support for the 5-litre 'SS' model), the vehicle spun off at the moment of start-up on a wet and greasy road. He declined to support the 'SS' model.

With the demise of the 4½-litre Bentley, the 'S' model, capable of accelerating to 60mph from rest in fifteen seconds, was ranked as the most accelerative of British cars. From the mid-1920s the status of the Monte Carlo Rally had been growing, and the return of the event to a January date, a time when the motoring press had very little else to write about and therefore would tend to focus almost solely on the rally, made it that much more important to manufacturers. If the weather was kind it was easily possible for a touring car to win.

In 1989, Peter Garnier, the sports editor of *Autocar*, wrote a book called *Donald Healey – My World of Cars*. In it he wrote of Noel Macklin approaching Humphrey Symonds of *The Motor* to ask for a recommendation of a driver to compete in Continental rallies, which were often not far removed from road races. The recommendation was Donald Healey. The 'S' model was extensively rallied by Donald Healey, who was on a retainer contract by the company from 1930 until Invicta went into liquidation in 1934. He ran Invictas in the Alpine Rallies of 1931, 1932 and 1933. Donald Healey's successes included penalty-free performances in the Alpine Trials of 1931 and 1932. Charles Needham bought an S-Type which he used on the 1934 Alpine. H.J. Aldington, the managing director of Frazer Nash Cars said, when talking about Charles Needham, that the market for sports cars was limited to the wealthy and this year's hero would most likely be driving for a competitor the next year.

Many other wins came the way of the S-Type and, at one time, the model held the outright lap record for sports cars on the 'mountain' circuit at Brooklands. Donald Healey gained an outright win in the 1931 Monte Carlo Rally, when

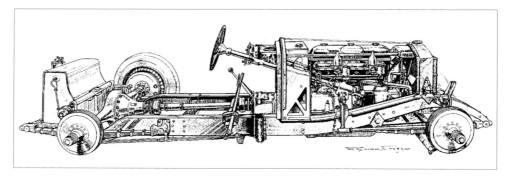

The Gordon Crosby drawing which appeared in the *Autocar* of 26 September 1930, at the time of the launch of the low-chassis 'Sports' model.

he took advantage of the bonus points by starting from Stavanger. Soon after the start he hit a telegraph pole in Norway, mangling the chassis and resulting in crab-like behaviour, which required constant attention to the accelerator and the steering. He said that this constant attention paid off on the difficult sections of the rally since he could not relax his concentration at any time. The following year he finished second in the rally with the same car, albeit rebuilt.

An S-Type (PL 5676) was built for competition and for promotional purposes. Raymond Mays, who was seeking a fast and reliable car after a disastrous season with a very special ex-works AC was also recruited to drive it in competition. This became, in effect, a semi-works car and the engine was extensively modified at the Meadows works. The resultant power output was raised to 158bhp at 3,900rpm. Mays went on to encourage the India Tyre Co. to purchase a second S-Type for the 1932 season (TL 2327). He used the opportunity to substantially improve the performance of the engine (transferred from the first car) and went in for significant weight saving. In the latter half of 1932 he was extremely successful at Shelsley Walsh. On 10 September there was an invitation scratch race at Brooklands for the twelve fastest cars of the year, in which Mays finished second to Malcolm Campbell's 4-litre supercharged Sunbeam Tiger.

Raymond Mays wrote an article for *Old Motor* magazine, published in the July/August edition of 1972, entitled 'Dreadnought on Wheels'. It carried the subheading: 'Easily the most reliable car I ever raced'. An extract follows:

> Low-built and short wheel-based, the Invicta was nevertheless heavy even by the standards of the period. But with its flat-riding steering and ultra-dependable brakes it was an enthusiast's day-dream on the tracks in the early thirties. My 4½ litre low-chassis

Invicta, in spite of modification and tuning to a point that its engine designer had never remotely envisaged, was easily the most reliable car I ever raced. I was well qualified to appreciate its unburstability, because its tenure of our Bourne stable largely coincided with that of the highly temperamental Vauxhall Villiers. It's true that the latter – supercharged and revved to merciless pressures and rpm rates – had plenty of excuse for showing the white of its eyes; but this didn't dilute our delights in the big Invicta's yeoman qualities. It practically never went to the starting line without winning or beating its class record, or both, and mechanical failures were foreign to its whole nature. The result, nevertheless, was a strongly characterful car of great aesthetic appeal, which owed its aggressive good looks almost entirely to Noel Macklin's personal influence. By winning the 1931 Monte Carlo Rally outright – this was the first time a British car had done so – the 4½ Invicta made world headlines. And it was shortly after this that I gained my introduction to the aristocrat of Macklin's mechanical family. I had been using India tyres on the Vauxhall Villiers sprinter, and Indias were standard on all Invictas. When, therefore, I contracted with Indias to fill the driver's role during a countrywide tour demonstration of their products in '31, it was natural that, Macklin's collaboration being forthcoming, we should pick on Invicta for our purpose. The car assigned to us for the India project, a 4½ litre open sports four-seater, specially finished in my own racing colours, white with pale blue upholstery, was mechanically standard and fairly 'woolly' even by the criteria of the day. Its six-cylinder Meadows engine, with a bore and stroke of 88.5 by 120mm, was low revving and rather heavy, and developed slightly over 100bhp. Its pushrod-operated overhead valves were in line, carburation was by twin SUs. The 4½ Invicta in untuned form was outstanding for low speed torque (it would pull smoothly down to 7mph in the highest of its four gears), and here we see a connection with an earlier involvement of Macklin's; he'd been fascinated by steam as a car propellant and actually bought and experimented with two American steamers, a Doble and a Stanley. He couldn't quite match their constant-torque characteristics with an IC engine but he had a darn good try! During the India tyre demonstration tour it occurred to Peter Berthon and me – Peter was, had been, and long remained, the technical brain behind most of my racing enterprises – that the Invicta's Meadows engine offered tantalising possibilities for development into a really potent piece of machinery. Consultations followed, with favourable results, with Capt Macklin and Mr Henry Meadows, the latter in turn bringing his chief designer, a Mr Crump, into the picture. The Invicta firm, it was agreed, would supply us free of charge with bits and pieces relevant to the proposed touring-to-racing makeover, while Meadows undertook to carry out the special machining, etc, called for by drawings of modifications that Peter Berthon would prepare, aided by that other fine engineer friend of mine, Murray Jamieson.

By the time Peter and Murray were satisfied, there were very few stress-bearing components in the engine that remained standard; conrods, pistons, and cylinder head,

Two photographs from an Invicta catalogue of the first S-Type with the new chassis and the steering box mounted on top of the chassis.

rocker gear, valves, manifolding and a score of unconsidered trifles for good measure, came in for the treatment. The conrods in particular were things of beauty, fitted with four bearing cap bolts a-piece and burnished to mirror finish. The crankshaft itself was almost the only major component that we reluctantly had to pass over, since a beefier one would have involved virtually an engine re-design.

Under the sports-car regulations of the day, for the events that we would be tackling, dope fuel was permissible, so the compression ratio was radically raised to exploit this. Finally, the hitherto 'woolly' Meadows was developing 158hp at 3,900rpm, which it would sustain reliably for one-hour periods on the brake.

Shelsley Walsh hill climb and Brookland Mountain Circuit events became the Invicta's happy hunting grounds, and her career at both venues opened auspiciously in 1931. At Shelsley, the very first time it ran against a watch the car tied with Tommy Wisdom's Frazer Nash for fastest time by a British sports car and won the British Championship Cup. Then, around the Mountain, a few months later, it broke the course record for its class (which didn't differentiate between sports and pure racing cars, blown and unblown), and finished second in its race in spite of the far from favourable handicap.

Here I must digress for an appraisal of the Invicta's handling characteristics and the design features that produced them. The car possessed over steer of a kind peculiar to itself, although the term over steer hadn't been invented forty years ago. Under cornering side thrust, it sat very flat on the track – it was almost uncannily roll-proof – and would take

The Ulster TT run of 1931 on the Ards circuit. Dudley Froy had entered his S-Type and had broken an arm in practice for the race. Motoring journalist Tommy Wisdom took over the entry and completed thirty laps to finish nineteenth overall. Due to the wholesale troubles in the class, with a Mercedes, three Bugattis, and Field's Invicta all pulling out of the race, Wisdom was first in class and the only one to finish.

The S-Type entered by S.C.H. Davis in the Mountain Handicap race at Brooklands, Easter 1931. Cushman is on the far left of the photograph. This photograph appeared in a number of newspapers the day afterwards, and was negative publicity.

Donald Healey competing in the 1931 Alpine Rally on the Engadine Pass.

bends of any radius astonishingly fast. Then, at a critical and unpredictable point, it would lose lateral adhesion like a flash and could be right out of control by the time you'd applied corrective lock. In those days, before the study of steering, handling and roadholding phenomena had become an exact science, we were I suppose far less critical than today's generation of drivers, tending to adapt ourselves uncomplainingly to our cars' quirks rather than calling on designers to go back over their homework.

Nevertheless, when I came to make my Brooklands Mountain debut with the Invicta I was very much mindful of the serious crash which Sammy Davis, contemporary sports editor of *The Autocar*, had had in a similar 4½ on the same course at the 1931 Easter Meeting. Turning right from the Finishing Straight onto the Home Banking, with the steep slope of this banking operating in her favour, he had 'used up' all his corrective (left-hand) lock and still not succeeded in bringing the outward-yawing back-end to heel. This, as Sammy was to declare in a published masterpiece of understatement, was 'odd to say the least'; so odd, in fact, that the car finally capsized and pinned him underneath in a grievously injured condition. I was to experience the same symptoms many times, though never, I'm thankful to say, with the same consequences.

But at Shelsley Walsh the same year the pendulum took a happier swing and the white Invicta yawned and clawed and skated its way to the summit in a time that undercut the next-fastest British sports car by a crushing seven seconds, winning me the British Championship Cup for the second time on the trot. It was here, at Shelsey, as long as one kept oneself constantly and tautly alert to combat that point-of-no-return over steer, that the flat-riding, hairsbreadth-steering 4½ paid its best dividends.

Loosely, I have referred to the white Invicta as 'my' or 'our' car, but in fact it was the property of the India tyre people throughout the period that I raced it. It was then purchased by my old friend Humphrey Cook, who was later to finance the ERA project that Peter Berthon and I had conceived. Humphrey, a public-spirited man but also a temperamental one, had been much impressed by our success with the 4½, and in particular by the car's phenomenal reliability in racing and hill climbing service.

It was in pursuance of the policy of appealing to a wider market that the small capacity Invicta was marketed in 1932. Wheelbase was 9ft 10in and it was powered by a 1,498cc (57mm x 97mm) six-cylinder single overhead camshaft engine,

The Charles Needham low-chassis car at Mainz during the 1932 Alpine Rally, in which Needham gained a Glacier Cup, having lost no marks.

Dudley Froy's single-seater. The Invicta prepared for record work and primarily the 1931 500 Mile Race but was not ready until the 1932 event, when it crashed in practice on a straight stretch of the Brooklands course.

The 1932 Mountain Championships. Campbell leads in the supercharged Sunbeam, Mays passes him and Shuttleworth in his Bugatti lies third; Campbell was to finish first with Mays second.

produced speculatively for Invicta by Hatch of Burney and Blackburne. In general design and appearance it was a scaled down version of the S-Type cars, with semi-elliptic springs and a lightened type of frame and lighter front and back axles. These changes materially helped the weight distribution. The initial model, the 12/45, received a great deal of adverse criticism for lack of performance, which was equivalent to that of the small MGs. If the axle ratio was decidedly low at 6:1, at least the acceleration in bottom gear benefited. The 12/90 was subsequently added to the range. This was the twin overhead cam version, which was also sold and used by Frazer Nash, and had a Powerplus supercharger, which gave a maximum boost of 15psi. Unfortunately, this model was beset with carburation and manifold cooling problems. It was only shortly before the company was wound up that a satisfactory supercharged car was revealed in prototype form. This was the 12/100, which had the cams geared together by helical gears and the valves set in the head at an acute angle. It was also to be available as the 14/20, which had a capacity of 1,660cc (60mm x 97.9mm), but neither entered production for use by Invicta, though they were sold to AFN Ltd for the Frazer Nash.

In the 1932–34 period the building of the Invicta was entirely carried out at Beverley Barnes workshops and they were also responsible for sending the cars to the coachbuilders, finishing the cars off and then shipping them to the Flood Street service area which was owned by Earl Fitzwilliam and where the servicing of customer Invictas was carried out. The sheds at Cobham were entirely empty and Macklin used the opportunity to try some freelance 16mm filmmaking.

The company's downfall came in 1934, when production of all models ceased and the 5-litre 'SS' model went no further than the drawing board. The 'SS' model was based on the '100mph' chassis, but the front springs were also to be mounted outside the frame, which itself was considerably stiffened by additional cross-members. The engine was basically the 4½-litre Meadows, but bored out to 4,890cc (93mm x 120mm) and with a new and very special twin overhead camshaft cylinder head and a supercharger mounted forward of the engine. Estimated power output was in the region of 200bhp and a chassis price of £1,875 was quoted. It was also rumoured that an 8-litre car was planned, but this over-ambitious project was later abandoned, possibly as a result of the lessons learned after the failure of Bentley.

After this, the works at Cobham were turned over to the finishing of the Railton, which was delivered from Hudsons works on the Great West Road. This was a much cheaper car, using a 4-litre Hudson engine, but the radiator bore more than a chance resemblance to that of the Invicta and there was the same rivet

Mays at Shelsley, driving the white Invicta (PL5676).

The 'Small Invicta' chassis with the 1,500cc Burney & Blackburne engine, fitted with a 6:1 ('buzz box') final drive ratio, and the five-seater saloon.

The last car from the Fairmile – the 12/100hp or 14/120hp – from the 1933 catalogue.

The end of the road – all parts and spares were moved to Flood Street in South Kensington, including the service van.

Charles Brackenbury driving a Type 51 Bugatti endeavours to overtake Bob Lace's Invicta, driving in the Mannin Moar race in the Isle of Man in July 1933. Richard Shuttleworth had just bought the Bugatti and was in the co-driver's seat. Lace brought down a telegraph pole during the race.

line along the bonnet that had characterised its predecessor. In the meanwhile, at the Invicta London service station, a few cars were being assembled under the supervision of Earl Fitzwilliam. Without the organisational skills of Cushman, however, the flow of cars never exceeded a dribble, and later ceased.

Invicta Cars Ltd, it was reported in late 1937, had made arrangements to sell, and later to build, a range of cars based on a well-known Continental make. The specification was said to be a box section and tubular X-braced frame. It was reported that arrangements were being made to reintroduce this car, deduced by the British press to be Darracq, to England. This was shortly after Comotti's TT victory. A Wilson or Cotal gearbox could be fitted. The specification included cable-operated Bendix brakes, four-speed gearbox, with synchronous gearing on top, third, and second. There were six-cylinder engines of 2,696, 2,996 and 3,988cc, with 75bhp, 90bhp and 140bhp. The 2-litre saloon was to cost £596, and the special saloon £695, with the Cotal gearbox option.

At the time it was thought that Invicta were definitely involved with this Darracq scheme, but this was never substantiated. Certainly Invicta Sales had discussions with Lago Talbot which also came to nought. A considerable number of Invicta owners had their names linked to this proposal including the Laces and there was also a rumour just before the war that a proposed Invicta was to be powered by an American V8 engine, but this sounds suspiciously like a deluxe Railton. Invicta Sales, having basically no financial funds behind them, had very little chance of bringing such deals to finality, since they did not have the drive of Noel Macklin or the organisational capabilities of Cushman behind them.

The sponsors of the Invicta had dabbled with so many different makes that there is a tendency to attribute to them at the slightest excuse various other makes. Neither 'Captain Macklin', as he was referred to in press copy, nor Earl Fitzwilliam had any connection with the Derek, a cheap four-cylinder 1,018cc or 1,247cc touring car, which appeared in the buyer's lists in 1926. It is merely coincidence that it was made in the Invicta works situated in West Norwood. Similarly, the Comet (presumably named after de Havilland's record-breaking aircraft), which was a four-cylinder 1,203cc sports two-seater, produced in 1936–7 in prototype form, had no connection with the Macklin Invicta Co. It was made by the Invicta Welding & Engineering Co. Ltd.

The Invicta story looked as if it was over forever.

FIVE

THE RAILTON

Noel Macklin was ever alert that if things started to go wrong he should look for another way. One can anticipate that he had been looking for 'another Invicta' since 1929, or certainly by 1930, and the Essex Terraplane 8 of 1933 was such an opportunity. He had to link Reid Railton's name to the product and launch the Railton. Reid Railton, who was canny, did not put in any money, but lent his name on a commission sales basis to the Railton project. He had to be convinced of various strategies, but during the life of the Railton car the business was profitable.

Noel Macklin was not averse to looking for funding in different ways; if a rich man approached him seeking to buy a Railton then Noel Macklin would suggest that the man should invest in a small batch of Railtons going through the construction and body building process and would be refunded his money with a small percentage for the investment when the batch had been completed and paid for. Hudsons required money upfront for all their work before the cars could leave the works on the Great West Road in London. Macklin recruited one of the richest men in England, Richard Shuttleworth, to become a director by investing £10,000 in the company – this sum covered the upfront commitments in purchasing chassis from Hudsons.

American cars during the 1920s and 1930s were designed for comfort, and this meant soft suspensions for bad roads and straight line motoring. The twisting, interesting roads so common in Europe were not so plentiful in America, except possibly in New England. American designs did not rate highly the requirement to go fast uphill through hairpin turns or downhill through corners on a bumpy road.

The Hudson Motor Car Corporation of Detroit in Michigan was a serious rival to Henry Ford. The Essex range represented its low-price offerings. Hudson had been founded in Detroit in 1909 and, from the beginning, was always a major player in the American car stakes. In 1924 the company sold 100,000 cars in the States and 34,000 Hudsons and Essex cars overseas. In those days the British import duty on goods manufactured within the Empire was significantly less than the normal import duty. Hudsons built a plant in Canada, so as to qualify for imperial preference, and this plant exported complete cars as well as some without bodywork. By 1933 they were in a position to ship CKD (Completely Knocked Down) cars to Hudson-owned factories around the world. The two primary European assembly plants were in Holland and Britain. Hudson imported 2,000 cars a year into their London plant on the Great West Road in the early 1930s, of which 200 were without bodywork, for bodybuilding by English coachbuilders.

In 1930 Hudson launched a straight-eight side-valve of 3½ litres, which in 1932 was increased to 4,168cc. This engine, 'seemingly' obsolete when it was offered, used splash lubrication rather than a full pressurised oil flow, but was incredibly smooth in operation and fitted into a chassis of remarkable torsional rigidity. The engine was not withdrawn from the Hudson range until 1952. This was the engine fitted to the Essex Terraplane. Hudson in England offered the complete Essex and Hudson brand range and it was late in 1932 that the 2,500cc 16.9hp Terraplane was offered with prices ranging from £275 to the British-bodied Windover at £299. The Essex Terraplane hid behind its rather tall, bold radiator a six or eight-cylinder side-valve unit, seeming to take up only about half of the vertical space, and having just one single-choke downdraught carburettor.

In April 1933 the Terraplane range was fitted with the straight eight of 4,010cc of 94bhp. The cheapest model available in Britain was an English bodied sports tourer at £365, which was remarkably good value. Noel Macklin had a warm relationship with his sister-in-law Violette Cordery and bought this new Terraplane for her and she rapidly became a strong supporter of the marque. For the 1933 Scottish Rally, held in early June, she was a member of the Terraplane Eight team which won the team prize.

Thomson & Taylors' workshops were only a few miles away from Cobham and the world of British motor racing was very small and limited in the number of people actively involved. Noel Macklin knew Parry Thomas and Reid Railton from the pre-First World War days of Edwardian England. Reid Railton was highly regarded due to his input into the *Bluebird* land speed record car, the Napier Railton, Brooklands Riley, and ERA suspension. He, with Ricardo, were Britain's most influential automobile consultants.

The first Railton of 1933 with bodywork by Freestone & Webb.

It was in June 1933 that the negotiations that Noel Macklin (no longer of Invicta Cars but the Fairmile Engineering Co.) had with Hudsons in Chiswick and with Reid Railton at Thomson & Taylors of Weybridge, Surrey, came to fruition. The Railton Terraplane was a logical follow-on from the Invicta.

The Railton was the first of what became to be known as the 'Anglo-American sports bastards', whereby a touring American car fitted with a sports body and limited tuning became a sports tourer. French manufacturers had done it earlier with two Delaunay-Belleville models and in Britain Lammas-Graham and the Brough Superior were to follow Railton. The formula consisted of a large understressed power unit propelling a lightweight car. This had been a successful design criteria since the beginning of car construction in the 1900–1910 period. Noel Macklin had found that it was easier to sell a big car than a small car. People with money could be talked to and convinced.

The following confirmatory letter was sent from Noel Macklin to Reid Railton. The letterhead was the Invicta heading but typed in were proprietors of 'RAILTON TERRAPLANES'.

30th June, 1933

Dear Railton,

The following is an Agreement we have come to-day:

No.1 That you will consent to your name being used in connection with the English version of the Hudson-Essex Terraplane chassis, which is to be produced exclusively by the Fairmile Engineering Company, and which will be known as the 'Railton Terraplane'.

No.2 That in consideration of the use of your name in this manner we shall pay you a royalty of £6.10 on every 'Railton Terraplane' or 'RT' chassis manufactured or produced. In the event of any other model of the Hudson- Essex Terraplane chassis, such as the smaller 6-cylinder chassis being converted in a similar manner and named the 'Railton Terraplane' we shall pay you on every chassis so produced a royalty, the amount of which shall bear to the sum of £6.10 – the same proportion that the retail price of the standard open 4-seater model of such chassis bears to the sum of £500.

Thus, if the retail price of the open 4-seater model of such other chassis were £250, the royalty payable to you would be £3.5 and so on.

The clauses were summarised of the agreement between Macklin and Railton: Reid Railton agreed to the use of his name in connection with the English version of the Hudson-Essex-Terraplane chassis, to be exclusively produced by The Fairmile Eng. Co., to be known as the 'Railton Terraplane' or 'RT' – sometimes rendered with a hyphen and sometimes not. As a consideration, R.A.R. to receive royalty of £6/10/- on every chassis produced, to be pro-rata'ed in the event of a 6-cyl version being built. An advance of £200 to be paid on signing the Agreement, to cover the first 31 cars. The Fairmile Eng. Co. to furnish a monthly statement of production. Before production of any Railton Terraplane commences, a schedule of all alterations from the standard Essex Terraplane to be drawn up. Subsequently all the cars to incorporate such alterations. Any further modifications to be agreed by both parties. Railton agreed to his surname being used, as Technical Director, on any notepaper, advertising or literature, and that he would give a 'reasonable amount of time' in an advisory capacity to deal with any technical matters.

Signed: A.N.C. Macklin

Witnessed: Elsa Starkey, Secretary

The eight-cylinder Hudson engine in a Railton. The air cleaner is missing but the Carter carburettor and Autolite distributor are fitted. The André, shock absorber reservoirs and dynamo controls are on the aluminium-faced plywood Railton bulkhead.

Noel Macklin found the discussions with Hudson in England to be beneficial in that Hudson agreed to build up the completely knocked-down chassis to the required level of specification. Noel Macklin had used his negotiating skills to see if he could get Hudson to fit his radiator, but this was rejected, presumably because it would be against Hudson company policy and might invalidate Hudson guarantees. Hudson would not install a lowered dashboard and a British-supplied radiator, enabling the chassis to be driven away from the works for final completion at the Fairmile.

Cobham's new product was officially entrusted to Reid Railton, or so the press were led to believe. The proviso that the modifications were to be minimal was Noel Macklin's, but there would be a new radiator shell and lower bonnet line as a minimum. The cars would all have specialist-built coachwork bodies and the chassis was to use Hudson wheels and brakes. Cosmetic changes designed to suit an upper middle-class market were necessary, and these included British electrics, instruments and steering wheels. The early Railtons used the American 6V electrics up to 1936. The handsome vertical radiator shell was designed by the *Autocar* artist, F. Gordon Crosby, to cover the Serck-made radiator. A strong belief

On the left is C.B. Thomas, the 'forceful and genial' Hudson Motors European manager with his wife sitting in APH 119, the second Railton produced. The next car is the first Railton saloon, a Ranalah, APJ 834, by John Charles. To the right of Noel Macklin is the Hudson chauffeur. A Hudson Terraplane is the fourth car in the photograph.

was built up in the motoring press that a considerable number of chassis design changes were implemented by the Fairmile team, but this, though never denied, was not true. Macklin was, no doubt, extremely gratified by these 'publicised enhancements'. A typical example was that the springs had been flattened to lower the cars and prevent roll over steer.

The cars were driven to the Fairmile with an unsupported steering column and a leather cover from the radiator to the driver. At the Fairmile the chassis, with the long wand-like steering column, was fitted with a lower Railton radiator, bulkhead and instrument panel to be then sent off to the selected coachbuilder and then to return to the Fairmile for electrification, road-testing and final commissioning. The Hudson radiators with which the chassis were fitted to drive to Cobham were presumably returned to Chiswick to be fitted to the next batch of cars.

From the beginning, Noel Macklin was clear that he did not want engineering to be carried out on the cars – if work was necessary then it would be put out to tender and the components required would be bought in. An example was the bulkhead and instrument panel. The fitting of Smiths instruments was more or less standard for all Railtons except the basic Sandown and Claremont models (later, the 10hp model, based on the Standard 10 chassis, used the Standard fittings). If Hudson components were used then words such as 'gas' were faced over with 'petrol'. Macklin and Cushman together certainly contained the costs which can overwhelm small companies when special work is carried out without proper authorisation. The only tools that were present at Cobham were a pair of wheeling machines to make bonnets and wings, together with a pillar drill and small lathe, which were tucked away in the coach house – these were remains from the Eric Campbell and Invicta period. The Railton had taken over the soubriquet from Invicta of 'rivets along the bonnet', but this was inaccurate, as Carbodies had false rivets and Ranalah often none.

In 1933 a letter appeared in the correspondence columns of the British automotive press. Sir Guy Domville, Bart, claimed that his inexpensive American car, a six-cylinder Essex Terraplane tourer costing just £275, possessed acceleration superior to that of any other car on the roads of Britain!

A counter-declaration from the owner of a supercharged 4½-litre Bentley was lodged, to the effect that no car in Britain could possibly out-accelerate his. The Bentley owner challenged Sir Guy to a run-off over a ½-mile standing start at Brooklands. The Bentley broke its clutch on the starting line; the car was repaired, and a re-run was arranged. The Bentley crossed the line first, but only by the smallest of margins. A Railton Terraplane tourer (which might be termed a 4-litre, straight-eight half-sister of Sir Guy Domville's car) was then put forward for a re-run. It beat the Bentley by three car-lengths, a considerably wider margin than that by which the Bentley beat the six-cylinder Terraplane.

November 1933 at Brooklands – The Baronet's Challenge. This was the second run over a ½-mile standing-start. Sir Guy Domville is in his Essex, R. Hunt is in a Railton Terraplane, Ivor Burt is in a supercharged 4½-litre Bentley, and there is also a Chrysler.

The chassis frame components straight from the crate, sent from Hudson's Canadian plant and assembled.

Autocar magazine said the car was ten years ahead of its time and the Railton advertising slogan 'It's quicker by rail – but its quickest by Railton' was born.

The Terraplane's high power-to-weight ratio, coupled with its high torque at low engine revolutions, rendered it effectively a 'no gearbox' car – exactly the guiding design option that Noel Macklin had always wanted. The gearbox design, with only minor modifications, was to be used in every Hudson-built car produced between the beginning of the 1934 and the middle of 1940. The 'secret' of this compact gearbox – and the reason why it was able to transmit the claimed 128bhp of the later Hudson Eights – was that it was built with very special SAE 3440 steel, which had three times the fatigue-strength of more conventional steels. This was established by Rolls-Royce at Derby, who were perturbed by the excellence of the Terraplane and its fractional cost compared to a Rolls-Royce 20/25.

Rolls-Royce at Derby regularly bought other makes of motor car to act as comparators. In September 1933 they bought an Essex Terraplane Eight four-door six-light saloon. In the same month, W. Lappin reported to E.W. Hives, then head

The Hudson Motors assembly track on the Great Western Road in London. The engine is a Terraplane six.

Richard Shuttleworth in 1935 having won his first major road race at Donington – the Donington Park Challenge Trophy. As a director of Railton Cars, he held one-third of the capital.

of the Experimental Department at Derby, on a run he had had in a Railton Terraplane. Lappin pointed out that the car was fitted with four Andre tele-control shock absorbers in addition to the standard Hudson 'Thermostatic' type, and he wrote: 'the suspension appears to be excellent for fast travelling and corner work'. The internal correspondence that developed between Rolls-Royce in Derby, the sales office in London, and the south of France, where Royce was living in semi-retirement, was revealing, and flattering to the standard Hudson-built Terraplane. Rolls-Royce admired the chassis build, smoothness, 'roadability' and quietness of the Terraplane. The one area of disquiet was that the road-holding at high speed in adverse road conditions was not good. In 1934 they bought the new Terraplane Big Six (same bodywork style as a four-door, six-light saloon) for further testing. By this time, 'Terraplane' was the marque name, having replaced 'Essex' at the beginning of 1934. The point that was made by Rolls-Royce managers, time and time again, was that the Hudson, selling at under a third of the price of a Bentley, was better value and a better car in a number of respects.

Pre-war Bentleys built at Derby had a number of chassis, road-holding, and steering deficiencies. The Derby engineers noted the sheet of heavy steel which reached from the rear of the frame to the engine of the Hudson was important in providing chassis stiffness. This fitting certainly improved the road-holding but was probably installed to provide a universal base for different body designs. This steel sheet was both the floor of the unit-steel body, to which it was welded, and the top of the frame to which it was bolted at twenty-three points. The unification of frame and body was the basis of the unit construction principle. The Hudson-designed cruciform-braced chassis-frame was not light by British standards but, as Barrie Price pointed out in *Rolls-Royce and their Competitors*, 'the Americans had found ways to lighten everything else'. The Terraplane was a completely unified structure which needed no structural help from the engine. It permitted the vibrationless mounting of the engine. Hives, discussing the excellence of the Hudson chassis in the Rolls-Royce internal correspondence, referred to the accepted American belief that 'an ounce of rubber was worth a ton of theory' – an idea which had yet to be understood in Europe.

A Dutch-registered Railton at the head of the Stelvio Pass in a preamble to the 1934 Alpine Rally. Reid Railton is sitting on the door of the car.

The Fairmile property in around 1935, with the Lodge on the main road. Just in sight at the bottom left and at the far end of the property at that time was a vegetable garden, to be replaced during the war by air raid shelters.

The brakes were unusual, being a mere 9in in diameter, though on the eight-cylinder chassis they compensated for this by being a full 2¼in width (producing a total lining-area said to be 172.7sq.in, or only 11.3sq.in less than those of the original XK 120 Jaguar, despite the latter's greater weight and infinitely greater speed potential). The brakes on the six-cylinder Terraplane were 1¾in wide. According to John Bond, the erudite editor of the American magazine *Road and Track*, the aim of the dimensions of the Terraplane's brakes was to provide a reasonable lining area which recognised the need for a low rubbing-velocity for the Bendix self-servo shoes. Reid Railton had a poor opinion of the Terraplane's brakes and of Bendix brakes in general. However, contemporary road-testers actually praised the brakes, considering them to be powerful, predictable, and well up to the car's speed potential.

Macklin was successful in his aim, as the on-cost of the Fairmile per Railton in 1935 for a batch of thirty-five cars was £12 per chassis, and that included the pre-delivery asssembly and service of the assembled Hudson chassis.

Inside the sheds on the Fairmile. Note the heads of the animals shot by Noel Macklin just before the First World War which had been brought out of the house to add verisimilitude to the film epic *Noel Duval*. Note the car with the Railton radiator fitted and a protective blind over the engine and instrument panel ready to be driven to the coachbuilders.

1935 University saloon by Coachcraft, built for Earl Howe.

The eight-cylinder Terraplane engine was mounted on the 113in wheelbase chassis. The aluminium body gave the car a total weight of 2,260lb and the favourable power/weight ratio produced some astonishing performance figures. The first Railton Terraplane appeared in July 1933, fitted with a touring body by John Charles, and this was known as the Ranalah. The acceleration, and a maximum speed of nearly 90mph for a fully equipped touring car, was available in a car costing under £500. Also available was a drop-head coupe, and a saloon, priced at £585 and £499. Ranalah's two-door sports saloon was an elegant offering: a low four-seater tourer with thin raked wings, cut-away doors, spare wheel mounted on the bath-shaped back, and fold-flat screen. The monogram 'RT' appeared on the radiator and hub caps.

S.C.H. Sammy Davis drove a tourer from John O'Groats in the 1934 Monte Carlo Rally, two Glacier Cups were gained in the Alpine Trial, and successes in minor events at Brooklands and elsewhere were achieved. However, Macklin was looking over his shoulder at the Roesch Talbots and the Lagondas, and was well aware that he needed promotional fillips. For 1934 the 28.8hp (4,168cc) engine, developing 113bhp at 3,800rpm, was fitted to the now 116in wheelbase Railton. The name 'Terraplane' was dropped from the Hudson and Railton models. Some

224 Railtons were built in 1934, the body styles remaining much the same, though chassis were available for special coachwork, the curious Skeffington–Smyth 'Grand Tour Coupe' by Gill being an example. The Railton was fitted with the Terraplane three-speed gearbox, which surprised British sports car enthusiasts with its small size. The Railton, like the Invicta, was primarily intended as a touring car and, although effective results could be obtained by 'hanging on' to second, it was a top-gear motor. Motor Bodies produced tourers, saloons, drop-heads, and at least one fixed-head coupe. Coachcraft and Carbodies, who were to be responsible for most of the Railton coachwork in the next few years, produced their first examples.

By the early 1930s, annual model changes, with the concomitant hyped-up advertising, were common to the American market, and the chief change each 'season' was that each individual model was 'improved' by getting bigger, wider, and heavier. During 1935, Hudson shipped over 100,000 units domestically and overseas, and made a profit of over $500,000. It was not until 1937 that the Hudson chassis became unsuitable as a sports body, but 1938 ruled out that option completely. The 1938 Railtons used the higher Hudson radiator. When in 1937 it became clear that future Hudsons were likely to be impractical for conversion to Railtons, Macklin asked Richard Shuttleworth to fund the purchase of a job-lot of Hudson kits of last year's model at a low price, said to be £100 each.

The Light Sports Tourer at home, with Lance Macklin in the car, 'Cushie' behind, and Noel.

Cushman at the wheel of the Light Sports Tourer for the 1935 October Long Handicap in which he finished second with a lap of 104.85mph.

In 1935 Coachcraft offered University and Stratton saloons (the Stratton being the deluxe version), they built tourers to special order, and in that year they produced their first Fairmile drop-head coupe, which replaced an earlier unnamed drop-head. Ranalah continued with the tourers and two-door saloons, Carbodies offered an upright four-door saloon and REAL were building a neat four-seater tourer.

Noel Macklin was always alert to the possibility of gaining further funding, to improve cashflow, by discounting a group of chassis to a client. Richard Shuttleworth, who was later to be killed flying a Fairey Battle during the Second World War, had funds beyond belief, and bought a 1935 Railton which was fitted with the Axleflex front axle made by the Bker Axle Co. of Cleveland; the beam front axle was split and a linked centre section incorporated to rival the ifs systems being offered by other manufacturers. It was never successful and was abandoned by Hudsons a year later in favour of the earlier beam. Richard Shuttleworth, having injected major funds into the company, was referred to as the chairman of Railton. He wrote to Cushman in December 1936 from his home at Old Warden Park in Biggleswade:

Dear Cushie,

Just a line to tell you that I was being driven from Cheltenham home, by my man Peacock, who used to work down at Brooklands, in the old black Railton. Through an error of judgment he hit a 10hp Morris car absolutely head on whilst travelling at 55mph. The Morris was doing at least 25-30mph so the difference in speed was 85mph!! We had a trailer on the back containing an aero engine being an all up weight of 10cwt.

The Morris was completely written off beyond repair, while the Railton was undamaged with the exception of one headlight, the aluminium fairing between the dumbirons, and two of those aluminium wheels. We put on two new wheels and drove the car home!!! We all hit our heads pretty hard, and I don't think it has done me any good, but it is a wonderful advertisement for the car!!

What I am writing to know is whether I can get hold of a 1933 type straight axle as I have never liked the knuckle type of axle. It was a bit bent after the accident mother had when she wrote off an Austin beyond repair and only damaged one of the steering arms, and now it is a bit worse, I hope not because the chassis is bent! I will send this car along next time it is in the vicinity and let you have a look at it.

I think I shall give up motoring until all roads are one way and there are no cross roads and Hore Belishas.

The weakness of the Railton, as understood by Shuttleworth, was that the wheels were never designed for brisk cornering, though, with hindsight, this does not seem to have been the case. Richard Shuttleworth was influenced sufficiently to have wheels made out of duraluminium which, because of rigidity, were less satisfactory than the steel Hudson wheels.

Peak production of Railtons occurred in 1935 – a total of 377 were turned out. A greater variety of body styles was available: three tourers by Ranalah, Berkeley and REAL, starting at £553 and 21.5 cwts. Two coupes were offered; one by Ranalah, and the other Coachcraft's popular Fairmile, which cost £633 and £650 respectively. It was in 1937 that the disadvantage of working up and improving the American chassis was brought forcibly to the attention of the Fairmile team, for the ever-increasing wheelbase and width of the Hudson chassis worked against the staid British view that you only made changes that did not inconvenience you. The 1938–39 Hudson cars had a remote steering column change, with reverse selected by the 'electric hand' (an electric switch mounted to the steering column to activate the reverse gear change). Railtons had to design a gear-change system to avoid the use of a steering column change.

Peter Crosby, who was to die in the war, drew and painted in a very similar style to his father, Gordon Crosby. This picture comes from a Railton catalogue,

In May 1935 George Brough, having previously made a Meadows-engined car with a pre-selector gearbox, offered the new Brough Superior, based on the straight-eight Hudson. Noel Macklin immediately blew the whistle for a foul and Hudson had to agree that Macklin had an exclusivity agreement for the straight-eight cars. A compromise was reached — George Brough would be steered by Hudson towards the smaller six-cylinder Hudson cars.

In 1935 the Railton Light Sports Tourers appeared and created much publicity. These machines differed from the standard Railton in having the engine moved back in the chassis and being fitted with a higher rear-axle ratio — 3.56:1 or 3.3:1 — a Zenith carburettor in place of the standard Carter, and Scintilla Vertex magneto ignition. The Light Sports would reach 60mph in 9.8 seconds in road trim or 8.8 seconds when stripped — figures which few cars of the period bettered. They were fitted with four-seater doorless bodies by E.J. Newns of Thames Ditton. The very simple body, complying with sports car regulations, had space for four persons, and weather equipment. The body, complete with wings, weighed 1 cwt, and the whole car turned the scales at 19 cwts unladen. The car did have better brakes, and the design featured cycle-type wings, an external handbrake and a neatly rounded tail panel. A Light Sports Tourer was entered for the Ards TT. A high-ratio Marles steering gear was fitted, with improvements to the brakes, and double shock absorbers. The engine had increased compression at 7.75:1. The car did not run in the TT, probably for the simple reason that it was a prototype and not a production model and no similar Railtons had been produced. The price, at £878 was much more expensive than any other Railton.

The LST proved exceptional in terms of speed and acceleration. 'Phenomenal' was the word used by both *Autocar* and *Motor* (*Motor Sport* was content with 'breathtaking'). From 0–60mph took 9 seconds, and to 70mph, 13.6 seconds. The *Motor* achieved over 107mph and a ¼-mile standing start in 17.4 seconds. The car climbed the Brooklands test hill at an average of nearly 30mph from standstill, and leapt into the air at the top, covering a distance of 35ft before touching down. The extra performance had in no way upset the traditional Railton virtues of top-gear flexibility and good road-holding.

Only two LSTs were produced. One was raced by Charles Follett, and it proved to be an excellent all-round sports car. Specially tuned, it was capable of a 112mph lap speed on the Brooklands Outer Circuit. Follett made a good time at the Brighton Speed Trials in 1938, took the sports car record at Shelsley Walsh, and was close to putting up a new sports car lap record at Donington.

The year 1936 saw the Railton options from Hudsons of two wheelbase lengths – 120in and 127in – Coachcraft offered three long-wheelbase alternatives in the form of the Carrington drop-head coupe, a larger Stratton saloon, and a limousine. Their range was now considerably extended, for in addition to the larger cars, they also continued with the short-wheelbase Stratton and University saloons, produced two fixed-head coupes, replaced the Series I Fairmile with the Series II, and created a Light Sports Saloon. Carbodies produced a nice-looking tourer to supplement their newly styled Cobham saloon, and Ranalah continued with the tourer and two-door saloon (two versions being offered, one of pillarless construction) and introduced a new drop-head called a Sportsman's Coupe, which was a two or three-seater with unusual bodywork for the time – the tail and rear wings were one continuous panel. The Railton also acquired hydraulic brakes, replacing the original Bendix system, a remote-control gear change, the 'electric hand', and 12V electrics.

A 1935 Sports Saloon by Ranalah. (Peter Jane)

The 1936 sales took a downward turn to 310 cars, the Model 64 120in wheelbase Hudson chassis being utilised. Both sales prices and vehicle weights increased – the Carbodies tourer cost £598 and weighed 23.75 cwt. The Fairmile continued in Series II form, with Carbodies' Cobham saloon completing the catalogued 120in wheelbase range.

The appearance of the car changed a little in 1937 when a radiator grill with vertical slats replaced the earlier stone guard-covered honeycomb and the wire wheels gave way to ones of pressed steel. The wheelbase increased slightly to 122in and 129in. Noel Macklin had built the first Railton with a wheelbase of 9ft 5in (113in), a steering box gear ratio of 15:1 and a chassis weight of 17 cwt. Four years later Hudsons had moved on and the wheelbase was now 10ft 2in (122in), with a steering ratio of 18:1 and a chassis weight of 19¾ cwt. The weight increase was not that important – there was also an increase from 94bhp to 122bhp – but the greater chassis width militated against a sports car look and meant a much increased body weight.

Coachcraft's main change was to introduce the Fairmile, from which the external hood irons had disappeared, the Cobham saloon, which had fierce razor-edge styling, and updated versions of the long-wheelbase Stratton and

Carrington. Carbodies' Cobham became the cheapened Sandown (for £538) – costs were reduced by replacing aluminum body panels with steel, using inferior trim, and fitting the standard Hudson instrument panel (with 'Railton' labels in all the obvious places affixed with glue). Carbodies also offered the Claremont coupe in a similar vein. Coachcraft continued with the Fairmile, now in Series III form, at £688 and introduced their version of the Cobham saloon, again with the razor-edge styling then in vogue, for the same price. The long-wheelbase models, slightly reduced in price, differed in only minor details from those of the previous year. Berkeley and Ranalah were no longer producing Railton bodies but Newns offered a new drop-head called the Eagle.

The 1938 range, based on the Model 74, 122in-wheelbase Hudson chassis, continued much as before. The engine, with twin-choke Carter carburettor and better breathing, developed slightly more power. Body styles continued on the short wheelbase without a lot of change. From 1937, all Railtons were built on a special consignment of 200 1937 chassis that Noel Macklin negotiated at £100 each, though it was also said that the price was £200, which could be that Macklin was upgrading his option for others to hear.

Noel Macklin and Reid Railton had a meeting in the late summer of 1937, which led to a letter from Reid which was dated 23 September 1937. It is partially quoted for it is an example of the capability that Noel Macklin had for convincing people that they should adopt a course of action which may well have been foreign to their normal way of life.

> Dear Noel,
>
> I thought I would write to you, and so preserve myself from being over-persuaded by your honied words.
>
> It is still my view that I am being asked to make a considerable concession to enable you to pursue a course (I hope wrongly), I consider a poor one… However, in order to give the thing a chance, I am prepared…

These were disagreements concerning the introduction of the six and four-cylinder models in 1937, when Macklin tried to squeeze the royalties. Reid Railton complains of 'being over-persuaded by [Macklin's] honied words'! Matters obviously came to a head in November 1938, when a draft agreement, undated and unsigned, was drawn up between Railton and Hudson Motors Ltd. In a covering letter to Harold Reed of Hudson, Railton stated: 'I am perfectly willing, and indeed anxious, to continue with your company on the same basis that I have hitherto operated with Captain Macklin'.

A 1936 Carbodies Tourer. The two-door Sports Saloon with the backcloth of Brooklands. (Bryan Tyrrell)

Two new models did appear during 1937, and these were radical departures for the company. In October the 16.9hp model was released – it was based on the small-bore six-cylinder Hudson chassis and had a 2,733cc engine, which developed 76bhp. Two body styles were available, both by Carbodies – the Sandown and the Claremont. Costing £399 and £458, they shared most of the features of the larger cars. Performance was less brisk, as the weight was not much less than the eights, but a top speed of 70–75 mph and 0–50 in sixteen seconds was more than adequate for the time. In complete contrast to what had gone before, a baby Railton appeared, on a Standard 10hp chassis, with a choice of either a drop-head coupe, based on the Fairmile, or a saloon, which copied the lines of the larger Cobham. Developed, it is said, for Noel Macklin's daughters, the 'Flying Standard' chassis, fitted with a four-cylinder 1,267cc engine, was utilised. Both bodies were built by Coachcraft, the production being thirty-seven drop-heads and fourteen saloons.

Coachcraft continued with the larger ranges of Fairmiles, Cobhams and the long-wheelbase Strattons and Carringtons. Carbodies were now only producing Sandowns and Claremonts. Rippon Bros of Huddersfield built a magnificent limousine body on the Straight Eight chassis and dispatched it round the country, winning many concours events. Railton production began to run down and no new models were announced. The major event in 1938 was the introduction of the 21.6hp, six-cylinder model. This was similar to the 16.9hp, but had a 3,475cc Hudson engine, and was available in three body styles – the Claremont by Carbodies, the Cobham saloon or the Fairmile drop-head coupe (the latter two in the Coachcraft style but built by Whittingham and Mitchel). The larger engine, with 101bhp, provided a better performance than the 16.9hp, but only eighty-one 'Sixes' were produced in all. Other than the Coachcraft long-wheelbase Series II Stratton, other models continued as before.

The later Railtons were large fast-touring cars, whereas the earlier slimmer cars had been sports cars. By the time the 2½-litre SS Jaguar came on the market in late 1935 the market-share of the earlier Railton was fast disappearing.

Between 1935 and 1946 the Metropolitan Police owned twenty-seven Railtons, and the original Strattons gave way to the newer Sandowns. These cars were quite standard, with the exception of fabric roofs which where fitted to facilitate radio reception. Other police forces, such as Berkshire and Manchester, also experimented with the use of Railtons at various times.

On 17 February 1939, in a letter to The Fairmile Eng. Co., Reid Railton wrote: 'I understand from Captain Macklin that in order to provide further finance for your business, you are proposing to sell your business, together with the benefits of your agreement with me for the use of my name, to a company to be called The Fairmile Engineering Company Limited with a share capital of £24,000 divided into 21,000 Preference Shares of £1 each, and 3,000 Ordinary Shares of £1 each'. Later in April 1939 the new company was formally established. Railton later suggested: 'I imagine the purpose was to provide more capital for the construction of the prototype boat, which at that time the Admiralty had turned down flat.'

The SS1 and later the Jaguar SS100 were the death knell for the Anglo-Americans. With the Second World War in the offing, it was self evident that imports of cars or CKD kits from abroad would dry up.

In 1931 the Scott Engineering Co. Ltd went into receivership, and was subsequently reformed as Scott Motors (Saltaire) Ltd with R.A. Vinter as managing director and William Cull, an experienced and talented engineer, as technical director. Vinter was an extroverted, gregarious man who cultivated friends in 'high places', including, it seems, the Duke of Hamilton, Lord Louis Mountbatten, et al. He had a flat in London and frequented Skindles, the Maidenhead Thameside club and bar, very much the haunt of the 'in-crowd' pre-war. His presence in the London area was necessary to maintain links with the Admiralty and HMS *Vernon*, the torpedo research establishment at Portsmouth. It could well be that this is the connection that linked him with

The instrumentation panel of an open Railton.

Macklin and the Fairmile company. In an agreement dated 16 October 1941, Macklin sold to Reginald Arthur Vinter, of Mawcroft, Nether Yeadon, Yorkshire, 'certain shares and caused to be sold certain other issued shares' in The Fairmile Eng. Co. Ltd.

Few motorcycles were produced. Scotts concentrated mainly on Admiralty contracts during the 1930s and 1940s. Cull was responsible for various design studies in addition to this mainstream business, amongst which was a two-stroke three-cylinder car engine. Whether this was the engine in prototype form used in the Scott Sociable three-wheeler car is not clear, but it is likely. The engine had been conceived originally as a 750cc motorcycle unit, but one was fitted experimentally to an MG (or possibly a Montlhery Midget). Subsequently it was redesigned in 1,000cc form, and was launched in a new motorcycle. As few as eight machines were produced so, with modifications, one of these power units was installed in a Morgan 4/4. This served as a works 'hack' throughout the war, covering over 10,000 miles with little attention required. A 2-litre six-cylinder version was also built and tested for a short time in an Aston Martin chassis. There was some hope that this engine might have been taken up by William Lyons for the SS Jaguar.

Design work was also carried out on a 500cc narrow V-angle engine, with four bores in pairs, with a common combustion chamber. The usual two-stroke

DISCONNECTED JOTTINGS *By "The Scribe"*

Reprinted from "THE AUTOCAR"

August 17th, 1934.

Last week I repeated an experience I enjoyed to the full a year ago. I had the Railton Terraplane in my hands, the same car that I tried last year when I described it as being ten years before its time. I still think the Railton represents what motoring will be like ten years hence.

I was curious to re-try this car because it is such a light job for so large an engine; it weighs a ton, and has an 8-cylinder 4-litre engine, 500 c.c. per 2¼ cwt., and for the ordinary 1,500 c.c. 25 cwt. car to equal the engine-weight ratio it would have to be 7½ cwt., which, as Euclid said, is absurd.

Both S. C. H. Davis and I were of the opinion that with a car of so much power and so little weight a year's running would show whether designers were on the right track or not.

Since then that car has done 44,000 miles, has had new tyres at every 20,000 miles, and decarbonisation at the same time. Except for a spot of trouble when S. C. H. D. took the car to Monte Carlo, **it has only had 7s. 6d. spent upon it, and it has been driven by about 400 different people,** yet last week I found it

had less evidence of being secondhand than my own car, which is of the same age with only 16,000 miles to its credit. Its performance is now even better than it was when new, and except that the brake linings require renewing, one can say that it is just about nicely run in.

I have dreamed my dream ships by the dozen, but long ago I got tired of creating dream cars, until I tried the Railton Terraplane last year. Since then I have subconsciously made it my standard of perfect performance; it became my dream car, and after trying it again after twelve months' hard wear, it is still my dream car.

* * *

Dream Cars

One hears daily of terrific acceleration, and we literally mean that word terrific. A car with a terrific acceleration terrifies me. I always have a suspicion that the machine is the master of the man. But with the Railton one feels as staid and as steady as the driver of a Daimler Hire. It has three speeds, but for regular use one does not trouble about the intermediates; top is good enough for all ordinary purposes, starting, traffic, stopping and restarting even on hills, and accelerating when overtaking. One just strokes the accelerator and, without sound or evidence of machinery, the machine goes forward up to sixty in a second or so. Yet at no time is one afraid that one is going too fast for the road, so beautifully does it handle.

Last year I did not have to reverse and manœuvre about a garage, and last week I crossed my mind that I would have to be very careful indeed with the accelerator or find myself speeding backwards through the garage wall or removing other parts of it bodily. But I found that there was nothing of the fiery steed about the car; it behaved in a most lady-like way, and even when accelerating or carrying on at speed it felt like an aeroplane gliding with its engine shut off.

The glowing account of the Railton written by the scribe of *Autocar*.

The 1937 long-wheelbase Stratton model photographed in the Fairmile garden.

crankcase compression was replaced by supercharging, thus simplifying and improving crankshaft and con rod-bearing lubrication. Petrol injection was featured and an eight-cylinder version was to be developed for a proposed new Railton car for the post-war market. The Railton was to have an aluminium, aerodynamic body, but exactly what form the chassis and suspension were to take is not known. Laurence Pomeroy, noted technical editor of the *Motor*, is alleged to have had some input, and preliminary body sketches were prepared.

It was in 1950 that Vinter finally came face to face with the law. For years he had been juggling with the Scott finances, which had allegedly subsidised his style of living and financed dreams such as the Scott Railton. He was charged, tried and sentenced for malfeasance and misappropriation of Government (Admiralty) funds. He died in a Bradford nursing home on 7 May 1956 in somewhat reduced circumstances, having been living in one of the cottages that has once formed part of the family demesne. His estate was valued in probate at £4,559 6s 7d (say £60,000 in today's money).

On 30 October 1944, Reid Railton received a cable from Thomson & Taylor: 'If we buy up Railton Cars will you give us the sole rights to your name with your blessing?' Railton replied cautiously: 'Reluctant assent blindly your proposition without fullest details plans and financial resources.' Additionally, he took the precaution of writing to his solicitors in London requesting a copy of the 18 July 1939 deed to see where he stood.

During November, Reid Railton flew from London for a meeting at Hudson Motors, Detroit, in the course of which he verbally assented to Hudson proceeding with the use of his name, as he was under 'the impression that Macklin had now disposed of this to you [Hudson Motors]'. Obviously, neither party was aware of Vinter's involvement!

Reid Railton and Hudson Motors nurtured grand ambitions for the resumption of Railton production, involving the importation of Hudson engine/gearbox units and rear axles only, with all other components, including frames, to be sourced this side of the Atlantic. Railton visualised 'a good market in many foreign countries for Railton cars... such as the Sports Saloon and the

The 'Baby' (never advertised under this name but universally known as such) was a Standard 10 motor car with a more sporting body. This was Mia Macklin's seventeenth birthday present. Mia was Noel's second daughter and was a very advanced ice skater (see the mascot on the radiator cap), and she was present at the 1936 Olympics.

Drophead Foursome Coupe, which I would build in own shops'. Post-war austerity in Britain and the dollar/sterling crisis put paid to such aspirations.

In 1945 the business of Railton Cars was sold to Hudson Motors by Sir Noel Macklin for £2,500 seemingly without telling Reid Railton. Post-war, Hudson assembled a dozen cars from pre-war parts which were fitted with bodies by various coachbuilders. The devaluation of the pound against the dollar took the gilt off the transaction. The first offering, a Sandown saloon, appeared in 1945, and in the following year eleven cars were completed with drop-head and saloon bodies by Carbodies, Martin Walter, and Whittingham and Mitchel.

Two genuine post-war cars were built. One was released in 1949, having independent front suspension, an overdrive gearbox and a steering column shift. Costing £4,750 it had a drop-head coupe body by University in the Fairmile style. The last Railton appeared in 1950, again a coupe, by Airflow Streamlines of Northampton, and was exhibited at the Motor Show at a price of £4,168.

SIX

THE FAIRMILE BOATS

From 1935 onwards the future of the Railton was very limited, as the Hudson Co.'s proposed models for coming years were becoming wider, longer and more softly suspended. Noel Macklin's mind sought a new outlet. Vice Admiral Usborne's paper on the lack of naval preparedness in Britain was the litmus paper.

The creativity and capability that Noel Macklin demonstrated through the concept of making boats as if they were motor cars showed Macklin at his most brilliant – especially since the purchaser, the Admiralty, was opposed to the idea and only agreed when it was obvious that the nation needed fast launches, motor gun boats and motor torpedo boats, and that the Macklin concept was the only way to produce the large number required.

The arthritis which Macklin suffered was progressively worsening, and in the middle of the war was almost crippling on some days. Noel Macklin went to considerable lengths to disguise this from outsiders. Important meetings at the Fairmile were held in the house in what was known as the 'boardroom'. When people assembled they would always find Noel Macklin sitting at the table surrounded by paperwork, and would observe that he never rose during the course of the meeting.

The years 1900–1914 had seen the development of very fast and reasonably reliable and sturdy racing boats, mostly relying on the stepped-hull principle to enable them to plane on the water. The alternative was to plough through it. The main problem associated with converting this hydroplane stepped-hull type of craft into an effective torpedo boat was finding a way of placing the heavy but delicately controlled torpedo in the water so that it travelled in the right direction, at speed. The launching tubes used were those fitted in destroyers.

Noel Macklin in casual clothing on the first Fairmile boat, was built at Woodnutt's yard on the Isle of Wight (see Nada Caraman's piece on the form of his casual clothing).

The design breakthrough was the concept of housing an 18in torpedo head-foremost in a trough in the after end of a motor boat. An explosive ram operating against the head of the weapon pushed it backwards out of the trough, and when the motors tripped, the torpedo would continue travelling in the direction in which the boat had been headed at the time of launching. This device was satisfactorily tested in a standard 35ft motor pinnace, and in the first motor torpedo boat, designated CMB No.1 (CMB standing for Coastal Motor Boat). The danger of the boat running down its own torpedo was lessened and, although the torpedo would eventually overtake the boat it should by that time have assumed its correct depth, and be unlikely to strike the extremely small underwater portion of a planing boat. This was the intention, but it was realised that sea conditions worse than choppy could be, and would be, disastrous.

The success of the German submarine attacks in British coastal waters during the First World War led to demands for large numbers of anti-submarine motor launches. These were not available from British sources, and the need was met by the production of some 580 motor launches by the Electric Boat Co. of Bayonne, New Jersey, USA, which were shipped to the UK. Their design was based upon that of a type of motor cruiser popular in the USA. Early units were 75ft overall, but later deliveries were 80ft in length. Powered by two six-cylinder petrol engines, and displacing about 42 tons, they were armed with a single 3-pounder gun, sometimes with a Lewis light machine gun, and could be fitted with depth charges.

The first 40ft CMBs put into service were given a Lewis machine gun. The Royal Navy received seventy-two of this type between 1916 and 1918. These CMBs sank one German destroyer and played a part in the Zeebrugge raid. An encounter between six CMBs and a force of German seaplanes showed their comparative powerlessness against aircraft. Most were sunk, and the rest were interned when they sought refuge in Dutch waters. Their greatest achievements were against the Bolsheviks in the Baltic. CMB No.4 (now preserved in the Imperial War Museum) sank the Soviet cruiser *Oleg*, and a force of 55ft boats attacked Kronstadt, launching the only successful attack in modern times by surface craft on a fleet in a defended harbour.

Unlike Germany, Britain had made no provisions prior to the 1938 Munich Pact to prepare the Navy for a possible repeat conflict in the Narrow Seas – and indeed precious little provision to counter U-boats or pocket battleships, unless a battle squadron of cruisers were available for any conflict. It was inevitable that there would be serious, if not catastrophic, attrition to our merchant marine lifelines across the oceans if war broke out. The Second World War started five years too early for the German Navy. They had planned to build up a balanced

Vice–Admiral C. Vivian Osborne CB CMG, in a wartime studio portrait, which he presented to 'Cushie'.

navy that, by 1944, would have been strong enough to challenge even the Royal Navy's command of the seas. It was to be a corsair navy, composed of strong surface groups and a powerful submarine arm with which depredations on British trade could be made on an unprecedented scale.

Successive British Governments had been preoccupied with disarmament and appeasement, but the semblance of a large and powerful British fleet was retained. It was not necessary to probe too deeply to uncover weaknesses and shortcomings in essential categories. The British naval rearmament did not begin until 1937, but the Germans did not seem to have anticipated any such project in their forward judgements. The British rearmament programme was on a scale not witnessed since before the First World War and, within the industrial and economic capacity of Great Britain, the Navy set out rapidly and drastically to make good the deficiencies in its fleet.

The folly of utilising petrol as the fuel for light vessels was obvious to any sailor, but only the Germans took account of this. It was possible for petrol fumes to lie dormant in the hull of a ship and then explode in a catastrophic manner. The British, Italians and Americans all considered that if petrol was correct for aeroplanes, then the same anti-leaking and anti-puncturing procedures and systems would suffice.

The diesel engine development project carried out in 1934 by the Germans resulted in the adoption of a twenty-cylinder Daimler-Benz V-form unit – a high-speed diesel that was to give excellent service over the next few years. A second marine diesel was built by MAN as an in-line engine and was used for river craft.

The German Navy construction programme was based on light destroyers, which could provide a torpedo boat capability, and heavy destroyers which would stay close to light cruisers. The coastal protection vessels – S-boats ('S' standing for Schnell (fast)) – used the torpedo as their main armament (the British called them E-boats). R-boats, the German equivalent of armed motor launches, were used for estuary work. Armed trawlers completed the German inshore naval forces.

Reid Railton sitting behind John Cobb in the 1939 Railton-designed land speed record car with four-wheel drive. In 1947 this car took the land speed record at 394.20mph and confirmed Railton as Britain's leading design engineer in automotive and water speed records. (Sally Joslin, The Brooklands Museum)

ML103 – an A Type Fairmile of 1941. It was lightly armed but set up for depth charges or mine-laying. (Imperial War Museum)

Noel Macklin had served as a Lieutenant RNVR with the Dover Patrol operation in 1916–18 and knew about the problems of a war in the Narrow Seas. As a shore-based officer he would have been to sea in a variety of craft and seen and heard first-hand about any problems. He would have learnt of the liveliness of the American Elco 80ft ML at sea.

In 1938 Noel Macklin read an article from the *Seagoer* (a reprint of a 1936 article) entitled 'The Influence of the Submarine on Naval Warfare'. Its author was Vice-Admiral Cecil V. Usborne. The Vice-Admiral had a distinguished First World War record and, post-1918, was involved in various naval committees. He was the Director of Naval Intelligence from 1930 to 1932. This well-illustrated twenty-page article had been post-printed as an unillustrated four-page leaflet to be circulated widely in order to influence people – the intention was similar to Lady Houston's when she had attempted to energise public opinion in order to guarantee funding for the British entry in the 1931 Schneider Trophy races at Calshot by mooring her yacht off the coast at Calshot and fitting a giant electrically lit sign saying: 'Wake Up England'.

The last paragraph of the *Seagoer* article said: 'the submarine will take a position of greater and greater importance in naval warfare, and… the strength of navies must be assessed not only by the number of battleships, but by the number of submarines and the number of hunting craft which are complementary to them.'

Noel Macklin wrote to the Admiral asking if he would be prepared to arrange a meeting. Macklin told the Admiral that he had an idea for a hunting craft which he had been working on for some time, and which he would like to talk to the Admiral about. The meeting was successful, and Usborne called a meeting with Admiralty designers and engineers. They did not take warmly to the idea of boats being mass produced in wood on a flow-line basis, analogous to car production. Macklin and Usborne decided that they would set up the nucleus of an organisation which would be capable of putting the idea into practice. The idea was that various firms would mass produce specific components and dispatch them to boat-building firms, where the components would be assembled using tools provided by Fairmile.

The company was registered as The Fairmile Marine Co. (people may have thought that the Fairmile at Cobham was, at the very least, on a river, but this was not so). Admiral Usborne was to be one of the directors. It was decided that even if they could not convince the Admiralty, there may well be a market for their boat in foreign countries in roles such as coastal patrol, customs duties, fishery protection and so on.

The Admiralty declined to place an order for a prototype, relying instead on British Power Boats Vosper and Thorneycroft. These firms were not in the mass production business, but built vessels in the time-honoured manner. Macklin decided to proceed with the construction of a prototype vessel at Woodnutt's boatyard on the Isle of Wight, for which he would provide the finance. This was a private venture proceeded with in exactly the same way as De Havilland's Mosquito project and Vicker's post-war Viscount programme.

ML105 – a coastal patrol launch, converted to mine-laying in 1942, which took part in the Normandy landings. (Imperial War Museum)

Fairmiles on patrol. A drawing by F. Gordon Crosby of A Type boats.

A multi-page document summarising the Fairmile proposal was submitted to the Admiralty, but made no impresssion. Norman Hart, a leading British Naval architect specialising in boats of this size, was commissioned to produce designs. Reid Railton was sent to the USA to find a suitable marine engine, because there were none of sufficient power manufactured in the UK (apart from 'marinised' aircraft engines, and the availability of these would obviously dry up in the event of war). Reid Railton, on his return, was quite adamant that the Hall-Scott 600hp unsupercharged Defender engine was by far the best for their purpose. This was a V12 engine of 31 litres which gave 630bhp, or 925bhp when supercharged. After extensive negotiations, Noel Macklin obtained the 'sole concession' for the UK and Europe.

The 'works', where Invictas and Railtons had been produced, was immediately converted for an entirely different use. It was now dedicated to the series production, design and tooling of large hard-chine motor launches by using mass-production, pre-fabricated, water-proofed plywood, utilising the potential of 'non-strategic' industries such as furniture and piano manufacturers (the same idea was promoted later by De Havilland in relation to their Mosquito aircraft).

Macklin and Railton agreed that, with war inevitable, there had to be a powerful person in the United States to represent Fairmile interests. With motor sport clearly on the back burner, there were no real objections. The Admiralty agreed, and Railton, though appearing to be an independent, was a British civil servant in all but name. The British Government agreed about the necessity of having a high-level engineer to represent British interests in a world of innovative American engineering, and Railton became the person on the spot to monitor such developments. Vosper required engines too. After a year with the Hall-Scott engine and the requirement for more engines than Hall-Scott could produce, it was inevitable that the high-powered Packard boat engines would become necessary. In the mid-1940s, Packard also produced the Rolls-Royce Merlin for the Mustang and other aircraft.

During those inter-war years, the only powerful British marine engine being made in any numbers was the Thorneycroft RY12 using petrol fuel, which had been developed from the 1918 CMB engine to produce a maximum of 650bhp. The Admiralty ordered ten in the 1920s and 1930s, six to be fitted in two 75ft motor minesweepers and the other four to power wireless-controlled target boats. Scott-Paine (British Power Boat Co.) tried to interest the Admiralty in a design of a small MTB (60ft length and 20 tons displacement) with two torpedo tubes, rated 29–30 knots at a continuous maximum rating. They were to be built with hard-chine wooden hulls and decks of aluminium alloy sheet. Approval was given and two flotillas constructed and commissioned. The engines used were Napier Lion (petrol-powered aircraft engines, marinised), capable of 450bhp on a continuous rating and a maximum of 600bhp, with three engines per boat. Considering their small size these boats were reasonably successful, and they were good sea-boats at moderate speeds, although sometimes sustained broken frames if driven through rough seas. The decks also suffered from corrosion trouble and had to be re-decked with double diagonal mahogany planking. Scott-Paine's business rival and competitor, Peter Du Cane of Vosper, built a private-venture MTB (which later became the Navy's MTB 102, achieving fame at Dunkirk), in 1935–36 – the engines fitted were three Isotta Fraschini 1,050bhp (continuous maximum rating). These 57-litre Italian engines had been in development since 1929, specifically as high-power marine engines for the Italian Navy, in order to replace their usage of the marinised Napier Lion. However, the Italian Navy carried on with the Lion for many years – spare part orders to Napier were still being placed in the 1950s.

The outcome was that the Admiralty decided to purchase the Vosper boat and use her for further trials and experiments with various armament fits. She was commissioned in 1938. During these trials all personnel involved became enthusiastic about the Isotta engines, and when the building programme was planned the Admiralty ordered three dozen engines for the twelve boats.

ML129 – a B Type boat. (Imperial War Museum)

Scott-Paine also built a private-venture boat, hard-chine, a fraction over 70ft, very beamy at nearly 20ft and powered by three Rolls-Royce Merlin engines which he had persuaded Rolls-Royce to marinise. Each engine gave 1,000bhp at 3,000rpm (emergency rating). Following trials of this boat, Scott-Paine shipped it over to the USA to take part in a competition for various types of MTB organised by the US Navy. This British Power Boat behaved well, giving a performance of the same general order as its Vosper rival; similarly to that rival, the high speed trials led to the need to strengthen the hull structure by adding stiffening in the appropriate places. Scott-Paine gained a contract with Rolls-Royce for the supply of marinised Merlin engines for future installation in the MTBs which the firm was then building for foreign navies (France and Sweden). One outcome of the US trials of this PV70 boat was that it formed the prototype for the US Navy's own Elco 70ft PT boats, fitted with three Packard 4M2500 engines and US armaments. Not quite what the British entrants had foreseen as the result.

Packard had, before the war, designed and built their own 2,500cu.in (40.8 litres) engine for marine use giving a maximum of 1,350bhp in supercharged form. In March 1939 Packard announced the acceptance of a $2million contract from the US Navy for production of the 4M V12 marine engine. In September

1939 Hubert Scott-Paine visited Packard to place a contract for large numbers of these engines. Packard also later built the Rolls-Royce Merlin engine under licence for aviation use, but Beaverbrook stipulated that the Merlin was solely for RAF use. It was as a result of this that Merlins found their way into RAF air-sea rescue boats, and this was not Beaverbrook's intention.

After the Munich 'crisis' the Admiralty began to take a renewed interest in the activities of the Fairmile Marine Co. and, in the early part of 1939, Noel Macklin and Admiral Usborne were requested to attend a further meeting at the Admiralty to elaborate on Noel's plan. The meeting was presided over this time by the Third Sea Lord and Controller of the Navy, Admiral Sir Bruce Fraser, who had with him representative officials of all the technical departments. After this meeting and further discussions, the Fairmile Marine Co. published a paper which defined the objectives given at a luncheon at the Hyde Park Hotel on 17 August 1939. Following that meeting a second submission was made to the

ML136 operating out of Lerwick, 1942, in camouflage for operations in the Norwegian fjords. (Imperial War Museum)

Fastening double thickness bulkheads.

Transoms, completely prefabricated.

The bulkheads are assembled on jigs.

Keel members prepared for assembly.

Bulkheads in the assembly shop.

Close seam work, trueing plank edges.

Production of the wooden components of the D Type Fairmiles gets under way. Reprinted from the *Motor Boat and Yachting* of August 1943.

Admiralty which was based on the belief stated in the opening paragraph of the paper: 'The Fairmile Marine Company has been formed for one purpose, that of building Anti-Submarine vessels to deal with submarines and of building them on a quantity basis by a specialised plan in the event of an emergency arising.' As the years went by craft were built for convoy work, mine-laying, mine-sweeping and various armoured roles and as in the capacity of MTBs and MGBs.

The key sentence was: 'Our scheme is in its nature the antithesis of accepted mass production methods... we decentralise the execution of the work... by putting out the various components to firms who are each specialists... and the assembling to Yacht or Ship Yards, which again are specialists.'

The vessel was half-built at Woodnutt's yard in the Isle of Wight, when it was obvious that war was inevitable. The Admiralty, deciding that the method of construction was not only 'sound', but the only way to build boats in large numbers, placed an order for twelve vessels. This Norman Hart-designed 110ft craft became the Fairmile 'A' Type, and the first was completed for trials in March 1940.

The sheds on the Fairmile which had witnessed the construction of Invictas and Railtons now became a prototype design studio to create the jigs and fixtures for the production and, as the years went by, the number of staff, mainly draughtsmen and women, at the beginning were increased to cope with the logistical paperwork demanded by the Admiralty for processing orders placed on boat yards and accounting purposes. As the war developed training for crews took place on the Fairmile with the components of the boats on display and an engine and transmission line which could be started up. Of the 500-plus people employed by the Fairmile Marine Co., over 200 were in-house on the Fairmile, with many hundreds out in the forty-five shipyards and eighty-seven slipways building the Fairmile boats.

Capital was required. Noel Macklin was unable to provide this and a creeping nationalisation programme occurred, but Noel insisted that the Lodge leading onto the Fairmile property was retained as his private property. The Fairmile Co. continued to carry on the business under an agency agreement, thus retaining independence from the Admiralty, keeping its original name, and receiving contracts from the Director of Navy Contracts which permitted it to make a profit. The staff made its purchases to the best advantage, and overheads, such as design, buying, supervision, handling, and a spare parts service, were kept below 4 per cent. Noel Macklin stated that he would carry on as the MD, but did not want a salary; the Admiralty insisted that he was paid and it was finally settled at a rate of £1 per year. Nevertheless he was to share in the profitability of the company.

Hall-Scott's V12 Defender engines powered the A, B and C Type Fairmile boats.

Reid Railton became an employee of the Admiralty as they recognised the wisdom of having a man in America to represent them in engineering matters. For Vosper he obtained Hall-Scott engines, since the Italian Isotta Fraschinis were not available. As the war progressed Railton persuaded Thomson & Taylor to start overhauling engines for the Admiralty in order to save precious dollars. T&T, as they were generally known, took over the Packard engines as well, and at Brooklands they were operating a bonded warehouse-cum-overhaul facility.

To ease their increasing workload Fairmile sought capacity from other industries. A linoleum manufacturer turned all the shafting, wire netting manufacturers provided rudders, a bell foundry cast propellers and Sercks, a large radiator company, constructed the fuel tanks. Cutting the material for the hulls was entrusted to a substantial timber merchant at Brentford. Brentford was also home to the central stores where everything connected with the hulls was delivered from outside contractors, and where the sets of parts were made up as kits and despatched to the large number of boatyards engaged in the construction of Fairmile designs. The non-wooden 'hardware', including engines and machinery installation equipment, was kept in 'No.4 Store', within the perimeter of Brooklands, part of Thomson & Taylor.

Macklin recruited personnel. Lawrence Cushman – 'Cushie' – from the Invicta and Railton days, was manager and later became the senior director of the company on site. His main activities involved specifiying and purchasing. When the war started Admiral Usborne also had an office on the premises. Noel Macklin had learnt the lesson that people involved in motor racing were good at extempore design, and fast in reacting to circumstances. He looked down the road to Brooklands, which he had known since 1910, for staff.

The Admiralty knew of the design revolution that had taken place in the RAF with power-operated turrets, and they contacted Archie Frazer-Nash at Nash & Thompson of Tolworth to canvass his views on the suitability of powered turrets at sea. They had carried out only limited work for any organisation outside the RAF (the exception was for the Army with the Matilda tank, which incorporated the Nash & Thompson hydraulic motor for horizontal and vertical traverse. When Archie Frazer-Nash visited the Fairmile and found that Cushie was in charge, they practically fell into each others arms in joyful reunion. One Admiralty design engineer on the premises made a secret report querying the relationship between the two, but the friendship between the two men was over thirty-five years old, and the fact they had raced at Brooklands together and won important races was regarded as sufficient reason for their pleasure in each others company.

Left: This photograph was taken from the after port side of the bridge of a C Type Fairmile MGB. This photograph was much reproduced to show the happiness of the gunner in his Vickers 'tub' – a Frazer Nash hydraulically powered gun turret with twin Vickers .303 machine guns.

Below: As the war went on the armament of the MGBs started to include Frazer Nash hydraulics, powering Oerlikon guns and later twin Oerlikons. Here on trial at the Shoeburyness testing grounds.

Archie Frazer-Nash was asked whether he thought his aircraft gun turrets would work in the harsh environment of salt-laden sea spray. He said: 'there is one way to find out and that is to dunk one in the sea and then let it dry out, perhaps do it three or four times.' When asked 'Well did it work?' the reply was: 'Of course it didn't, but when we had redesigned it, it did.' His aeroplane turrets were hydraulically powered so that the operator, irrespective of external conditions, could turn, track, raise and lower the gun by hand pressure. The first powered Frazer Nash gun turrets were installed in MTB 102 made by Vosper and were described as Vickers turrets by Frazer Nash's firm, because they mounted two Vickers 0.5in machine guns. The Navy referred to the turrets as 'tubs'. The FN5, used as front armament for a host of aeroplanes, including Wellingtons, Stirlings, Sunderlands and Lancasters, was the principal naval turret. The FN7 – a deeper, slimmer turret which achieved recognition carrying a searchlight for night-time sub-hunting by aeroplanes – was adapted for naval use. Frazer-Nash became very involved and a subsidiary of his Nash & Thompson gun turret company – The Marine Mounting Co. – was formed with works at Broughton, near Swindon.

The powered mountings based on the RAF Mk5 and Mk7 turrets came into service in July 1940 and continued up to the end of 1943 when the 1943 Class boats came into service with Oerlikons on Frazer-Nash-designed powered mounts. The powered Oerlikon was retro-fitted in some boats completed prior to July 1940. Enclosed powered turrets of the RAF type had been tried, but led to sickness of the operators, and condensation on the plexi-glass did not help viewing.

Charles Mortimer was born in 1913 and was a motorist, firstly with motorcycles and then cars. He was buying and selling and all the time he competed in motor racing. His book, *Brooklands and Beyond*, was published in 1974 and has a considerable amount of space recording his 1939 memories:

It was time now to get down to the question of what I was to do, I had no feeling of gallantry, but had a strong desire to make a contribution to the war effort – but very little idea of what I could do best. I saw a lot of both George Harvey Noble and Charlie Martin at this time. Both were Brighton residents and close friends but, of the three of us, only Charles really knew where he was going and that was into the Navy. Many friends were waiting and marking time in the Auxiliary services. Jock Forbes was in the Police Force in town and George Lane, a superb motoring artist, had joined the fire service.

Then Jock rang me and said he was leaving the police and taking a temporary job at Cobham with the Admiralty and, if we could meet, there could be something for me. By the time we met, a week later, Jock was in his new job and we discussed it over lunch at the White Lion at Cobham.

His first action was to obtain the services of Carol Holbeach who had been Sales Manager of T&Ts and had been based at their depot in the Paddock at Brooklands. Carol's job had come to an end with the outbreak of war and I knew him well for, in my 'dealer' capacity, I had done odd transactions, mostly involving rather cheap and tatty cars that T&Ts had had to take in part exchange when supplying new Railtons.

The first task that Noel Macklin gave Carol was to make a coastal motor-tour round England, Scotland and Wales and return with a list of small boatbuilders, now out of work because of the war – 'and please be back here with the list, within a week'.

On his return, which took a little more than a week, Carol, who had had no sleep at all and was looking forward to a day or two's relaxation, was met with: 'Now will you do the same thing again. Not boatbuilders this time. Small machine shops, even garages with machining capacity, who are in the same position, with no work on hand. Many thanks, see you in a week.' Somehow, poor old Carol managed to do this, too.

Noel was away signing up the boatyards all round the coast taken from Carol's list. He had negotiated arrangements with Hudson Motors on the Great West Road at Chiswick, and with T&T so that they now had two vast stores. Hudson's was to be used for storage and shipping out of all metallic parts, other than engines. T&T's new building at Brooklands, into which the marine fittings of the boat did initially pour, direct from the garages and the machine shops, took over the responsibility of handling the Hall-Scott engines and spares...

There were a number of well-known names within the organisation. Dennis May, the well-known motoring and motorcycling journalist was in charge of the big store at Brooklands, 'Jumbo' Goddard whose lovely cars now grace the Vintage scene was an outside engineer and Granville Bradshaw of ABC fame was also involved, to name but a few.

Some of the loads themselves involved ingenious planning. The keel used to go out in a number of sections on one load, on big 15-ton rigid eight-wheelers, while the frames and bulkheads followed on another, a week or so later. Planking would continue and then would come the marine fittings. The funnel of the 'B' boats was a problem – it measured 12ft by 6ft by 4ft and being light and bulky it didn't want to fit in any load although we tried many different permutations in an endeavour to economise as much as possible in the use of transport. Jack solved this one with the bright idea of wangling two funnels at a time into a 1,000ft capacity furniture van and it was at this point that we met a wonderful friend.

Gurney Smeed owned a small transport business. 'You'll never find me, you see. There are three chaps in my business – Mr Gwilt, Mr Smeed in the office, and the driver.' He did wonderful work for us. Runs to Scotland which used to take many drivers a week before we saw them again would take him three days, if the pressure was on. He became known to many of the crews of Fairmile boats at their Naval bases and if he arrived late there was always something for him to eat and a bunk on board for the night. Like Jock and I, he remained with the organisation throughout.

The 'B' Type Fairmiles had two American Hall-Scott twelve-cylinder petrol engines and these we carried crated. They were 9ft long and nearly 5ft wide in their crates and since our insurance limit was $20,000, we could carry four at a time on a 15-tonner at their value, apiece, of $5,000. Carried crosswise, they made an impressive load – one felt that one was getting value for money when four Hall-Scotts left for Scotland!

When the contract came along for the 'D' Type boats, the Hall-Scotts were replaced by four Packards of identical value, per boat. It was just possible to cram five of these big engines on to a 15-tonner, but we weren't allowed to do it because of the insurance ceiling.

One of the best things about the Fairmile job was the encouragement and support we had from both Noel Macklin and Carol Holbeach in cutting through red tape.

The Admiralty had backed the design of the hard-chine A Type ML but soon decided that it was not quite what was required – it was not fast enough at 22–25 knots to be an MTB, and not robust enough to be an all-purpose boat. The Admiralty at this stage (1939–1940) had approved the mass production techniques inspired by Macklin's genius and asked Fairmile to cooperate in producing a more seaworthy boat of about the same size as the A Type, which would be more capable of dealing with heavy seas. They required a more seaworthy boat of about 20 knots, but capable of more all-round duties, and the Admiralty commenced experiments in the Haslar test tank at Gosport, where the lines were established. The Admiralty designer W.J. Holt came up with a round-bilge hull design, and Sydney Graham was employed by Fairmile to draw up the details. The new motor launch became the two-engine Fairmile 'B' due to the shortage of engines; it was therefore slower than the 'A' but of much improved design, and during the war some 592 B Types were constructed, either in UK yards or from kits sent out to various ports abroad. The Canadians built a further eighty. The B Type ML was originally intended to have triple screws, but Hall-Scott could not provide their Defender engines fast enough to cope with the Admiralty's demand for more and more boats in a hurry. The urgency stemmed from the unexpected speed of the German advance in 1940 and the fall of France, coupled with German occupation of all the Continental North Sea, Channel and Brittany ports. The result was a twin-screw boat.

It had a sickbay of about 10ft square on the quarterdeck with 4 bunks. The galley was about 8ft square with a coal-burning cooking range and a guardrail, known as a fiddle, to stop saucepans falling off. There were fourteen crew, including two officers and, for a short time, the First Lieutenant was an eighteen-year-old midshipman.

King George VI inspected the invasion fleet around Portsmouth, going from ship to ship in a B Type Fairmile – RML 529 – mounting the Royal Standard. The King congratulated the RNVR lieutenant on his boat and heard, so it has been handed down, that 'it was no thanks to the Admiralty but one man, Noel Macklin, that the Navy had these boats at all'. Shortly afterwards Noel Macklin was knighted.

In the early stages of the war the B Types were relatively lightly armed, often with a pre-First World War 3-pounder 'goose gun' on the fore-deck. As the war went on, armament was stepped up as it became available. Some of the B Types operating in the 'chaungs' in the Malayan theatre were quite heavily armed as MGBs with 2-pounder pom-poms, Oerlikon and the occasional 40mm Bofors, to upset the Japanese army units. The low speed of the B Type was no handicap in the congested waters of the 'chaungs' – the low speed and quiet exhausts were a positive advantage in those conditions.

Many B Types were fitted with the excellent Type 970 radar prior to Operation Neptune in 1944 to act as pinpoint navigational leaders before the landing craft went in to the D-Day 'Overlord' beaches, and some B Types also took part in the 'spoof' landings off the Pas de Calais, as electronic 'spoofer' transmitters.

Many Fairmiles were also fitted with mine-sweeping gear of various kinds and did valuable work off the Normandy beaches in the months following the June 1944 D-Day landings. That the B Types were so versatile, being able to perform such a range of different duties, was due to the foresight of Noel Macklin, Sydney Graham and William Holt who, from the very early days of the B Type's production, arranged for all the builders chosen to finish a 'B' from the kit supplied, and to fit the upper deck with a variety of steel plates and strips, each one drilled and tapped in the right places and with the correct screw threads to suit the base securing bolts of different sorts of equipment (including the torpedo tubes removed from some of the fifty ex-American destroyers acquired early in the war, the depth charge chutes, the Holman projectors, the pom-pom mountings, the mine rails and a range of powered gun mountings). That forethought enabled a 'B' to have its operational role changed with only three days notice (sometimes less). If the need arose, the process could just as quickly be reversed.

By 1944 the Navy had many D Type boats. This one, a gunboat, has had its number removed by a zealous clerk for security/press release purposes. The boat was typical of its period in that D Type boats were no longer necessarily torpedo carriers but mainly gunboats. This one, seen here in the English Channel, went out to the Adriatic to upset German troop movements and services from Italy to Yugoslavia.

The B Type boats were built on wooden frames in the same manner as the A Type, with fore and aft stringers and intermediate prefabricated bulkheads – this was far from the traditional way to build a boat. However, because the bulkheads were supplied pre-cut and shaped, the builder had little scope for error, as that was required once the bulkheads had been accurately secured and plumbed into their correct spacing to run the stringers through. The B Type boats saw multifarious uses as the war went on – primarily convoy escort work up and down the east coast routes in the North Sea throughout the war and escort duties off the north coast of Africa from late 1942 onwards. A number were fitted with Asdic and an outfit of depth charges, so they could be used on anti-submarine duty. The forethought which went into the design of the Fairmiles enabled thirteen B Type Fairmiles to have their armament removed and a large deckhouse bolted on aft of the funnel so that they could be transferred to the Royal Army Service Corps in late 1944 as miniature hospital ships; the deckhouse was fitted up to take ten stretcher case casualties, while below decks the former wardroom flat was converted to accept ten bed patients.

The rapidity of the German advance in 1940 and the fall of France led to a requirement to provide defensive craft for our channel convoys. The craft needed to have greater speed and offensive armament than the B Types. The A Type jigs were available and the new design featured increased seaworthiness.

Haslar Creek in June 1944, looking towards Portsmouth. In the centre, S 317 is accompanied by two C Type Fairmiles – MABs 326 and 330. In the foreground are two D Types – 621 and 629.

The longitudinal stringers and the external rubbing strake of the hull were strengthened, the width of bridge and wheel-house was reduced, supercharged engines were used in place of unblown ones, fuel tank volume was increased significantly, the twin rudders were given a larger blade area (the A Type MLs had a very poor turning circle) and the boats were equipped with a variety of gun types. Three supercharged Defender engines, as well as heavier armament, were incorporated. All twenty-four of these C Types were completed by mid-1941, but their maximum speed was not comparable to the German E-boats. Nevertheless, the C Types had a very active war in a variety of roles. The were mainly used to strengthen the escorts for East Coast convoys by adding an outer escort ring with slightly more speed and a more formidable armament. Quite a number of 'C' gunboats were also seconded to 'cloak-and-dagger' work, landing and bringing back SOE agents and rescued Allied airmen, particularly from the Dutch and Brittany coasts.

What was needed was a boat that could handle heavy seas, and carry heavy armament. W.J. Holt's idea was to splice a destroyer-type bow – with sharp entry and a lot of flare – on to a fast motor boat hard-chine stern kit, with appreciably more beam than the A and C Types.

This apparently conflicting requirement was achieved by having the hard-chine of the box-like hull swept up in a smooth curve from just forward of amidships to the top of the stem. Exhaustive tests in the Haslar test tank gave very promising results, so the Admiralty approved the design, and the first prototype D Type was laid down in June 1941 and was launched from Tough Bros yard in October 1941 for sea trials. Those showed that the long, lean bow running gradually into the beamy hard-chine almost halfway along the vessel had, as hoped, reduced pounding when the boat was driven at speed into rough seas, and the boat was much 'drier' than other Coastal Forces craft tested, and was going to be a much steadier 'gun platform' for operational purposes. This first boat was fitted out and commissioned at the end of February 1942. During the rest of the war 226 further D Type Fairmiles were ordered, using over thirty boat-builders (two of which were Admiralty dockyards).

From the beginning, the D Types, known as 'Dog-boats', were given a heavy gun armament and, as the war progressed, that armament was steadily updated as more and better weapons and further power-operated mountings were developed and became available. The D Types were either MTBs with torpedo tubes or MGBs with heavy armament. The first two batches built were without 'scallops' moulded into the sides of the foredeck which would allow torpedoes to be fired. They were later fitted with torpedo tubes mounted on raised tube beds so that the weapons, when fired, could still clear the hull edges. All later D Types were

22 June 1945 — the Germans surrender three E-boats at the British concrete boat centre in Portsmouth. Their crews are coming ashore.

built with scallops, whether or not they were fitted with torpedo tubes, and were termed MTBs, since the decks were fitted with plates and strips in the same way, in order to provide quick conversions through the Fairmile method. As the war developed, the use of the 'Dog-boats' varied as to the theatre of activity. Exiled Norwegians operating as members of the Royal Norwegian Navy operated out of Lerwick in the Shetland Islands alongside flotillas of British manned boats. The flotilla system involved four boats – one would be an MTB attacking with torpedoes, and the other three would be MGBs which, as the war developed, were fitted with greater fire power. The Free French Navy in their D Types, after the collapse of the German Army south and west of Cherbourg in 1944, began to treat the coasts of Brittany as their own bailiwick. One crew put into Brest, which had been deserted by the Germans, to buy silk underwear to present to Lesley Cordery, Noel Macklin's second wife, and she, as a good French woman, gave them a mannequin display in thanks on the Fairmile.

The D Types were 115ft long and 110ft at the waterline. They did not have the yacht-like beauty of the earlier Fairmiles, but their solid nose and wider beam allowed them to operate in heavy seas. Power was provided by four supercharged Packard SM2500 of 41-litre capacity to give 1,250shp, on four shafts, which could be fitted into the wide after-hull. In all, 228 D Types were made (229 if the solitary F Type is included).

In 1944 the V1 flying bombs started to overfly Cobham on their way to London, but a number fell short. Consequently, the air raid shelters which had been hurriedly dug on the Fairmile site in 1939 were refurbished. Macklin called a meeting of all staff in order to tackle this new threat. He was standing in the main hall of the house and pointed out that, though the air raid sirens would sound, the only threat would come when the pulse jet of the V1s was heard or seen to stop when the V1s were approaching the site. He said that he had issued whistles to the air raid staff on site and they would whistle if they saw the V1s beginning their dive. He had only just finished this announcement when the shrill tones of several whistles could be heard, and the staff rushed to evacuate. Macklin, because of his infirmity, was not able to avoid the rush and was knocked down. He was not hurt, and laughed, saying that it was his own fault for standing in front of the main doors.

The Fairmile operation was involved in the D-Day landing scenario of Mulberry Harbour and outer floating steel-tank Bombardon, which were moored to buoys and linked end to end. King George VI had reviewed the invasion fleet in the waters close to Southampton and Portsmouth just before the invasion and was taken from ship to ship in a Fairmile boat captained by a young officer wearing his RNVR rank badges. The Royal Navy had more or

In the foreground is the German E-boat S221. In the background is a 73ft Vosper. Both are travelling at about 20 knots.

less allocated all the 'boats' to the RNVR, while the RN captained 'ships'. On the journey from ship to ship the King conversationally said that the young RNVR lieutenant must be proud of his boat and in response received a strong message that without Noel Macklin there would have hardly been any such boats at all. Within two weeks Noel Macklin was knighted. Various honours came to members of the Fairmile team, but not to 'Cushie', as it was established that at the time of his birth his parents had not been married!

As the war progressed and victory became assured, Sir Noel Macklin looked for further business opportunities. He decided that the Fairmile approach to building boats was entirely suitable for building prefabricated houses, using wood as the structural medium. A number of design proposals were presented to the Ministry of Health immediately after the war (in those days, before the rapid growth of Government, this ministry included housing in their remit). But Macklin in his lifetime could not have envisaged a sweeping Labour victory in the first post-war elections, which was closely followed by political rather than economic decisions. Hence the Government decided that steel, 'to help our brave lads in the steel industry', would be the key element, rather than wood. Macklin was not the only person quick off the blocks in meeting this 'opportunity', for about twenty firms submitted proposals, one of which was Scott-Paine's Power

Boat Co. of Hythe. This firm proposed a Fairmile look-alike in wood, plywood and insulation, named Scottwood. The company eventually built over 1,500 such houses. Macklin was too ill to react to this competitive challenge.

A total of over 800 Fairmile boats were produced (including the special variants built for Combined Operations), of which over 500 were built in UK yards. The remainder were built by yards in Egypt and the Far East from kits of parts sent out in merchant ships. Also of significance is the fact that Marine Mountings of Swindon, having fitted their guns and 'turrets' to the Fairmile boats, now had their designs fitted to other coastal craft. The company produced 821 tubes for the twin 0.5 Vickers machine guns of which 434 sets were made in the peak year of 1942. Around 2,500 twin-Oerlikon powered mountings were produced. Of the heavier weapons the 2-pounders reached a peak in 1943 with 228 sets and the 6-pounders in 1944 with 430 sets. The firm produced 4,155 mountings with guns (or turrets as they called them) from 1940 to mid-1945.

The Admiralty accepted the 'Fairmile way' – production geared towards flexibility and reacting fast to changing circumstances. This was completely different from the heavy-handed, 'dot-all-the-Is-and-cross-all-the-Ts' style traditionally associated with the Admiralty.

A painting by Keith Shackleton, for the *Motor Boat*, of a flotilla of D Type MTBs returning to their Christmas 1944 base in Ostend.

When the war ended the Admiralty received overwhelming support for Sir Noel Macklin's appointment as director of Small Craft Disposals — his job to dispose of (on behalf of the Treasury) the vast numbers of boats of every description built and commandeered during the war. This was extremely difficult, as each sale was similar to the selling of used motor cars. The Fairmile team, now headed by Cushman, carried on into the 1950s developing the Fairmile production concept, with a view to selling it on as a business.

Noel Macklin was almost entirely crippled by arthritis and Violette used to act as carer in order to get him to meetings in the Buick car they then used. As soon as peace arrived, Noel Macklin went to the south of France, where he found a house in Menton, hoping that the warmth of the sun would help him. He died out there and his body was brought back to England.

Macklin's obituary was published in the *Times* in November 1946. There was later printed a supplementary obituary written by 'F.T.B.T.' (this was Vice-Admiral Sir Francis Tower, who had held a communications role between the Admiralty, the Navy and the Fairmile. In this supplementary, Francis Tower wrote:

The end of the road. After the war many Fairmiles were sold off as house-boats and tended to deteriorate, as did D Type 783. The lessons learnt in the First World War about the intelligent use of Coastal Forces were soon forgotten and many observers think the same thing has happened post-1945. (Campbell McCutcheon)

His production methods were revolutionary in this country and in the early days there were plenty of sceptics. But not only were those prophets confounded, but the results achieved beat even Macklin's own ambitious aims. We should indeed have been in terrible difficulties at sea without the small fighting vessels produced by the Fairmile Marine Company under Macklin's direction and leadership.

Among his many virtues Noel Macklin possessed abundant charm. Unlike many men with first-class brains he was never impatient. He suffered fools gladly and was always ready to discuss difficulties and produce solutions, even when his own intelligence must have convinced him that the obstacles were trivial. No matter what problems were put to him, and there were many, I do not think he ever confessed that they were insurmountable. And in the event he was right. To his friends his loss is irreparable, and the country has never had a more public-spirited worker or one who gave so much without seeking reward for himself.

His funeral was on 12 November 1946 at Woking Crematorium, and among the wreaths there was one extremely large wreath entirely composed of violets. His ashes went to Bisham, doubtless spread on the grave of his father.

APPENDIX ONE

THE INVICTA POST-1945

Commendatore Piero Salerni introduced to the British market a hydro-kinetic power transmitter in 1937–38 and clearly licensed it to John Brockhouse, engineers. It had some wartime applications and a Humber car was so equipped during the war.

During the war and after Noel Macklin's death, work had been proceeding on a new and very advanced Invicta in premises in Hounslow, just off the Great Western Road, in London, led by Messrs Mabley and Kallenbourn, a firm whose engineering connections had sprung up with the war and were within the aircraft industry. Frederick Mabley had known William Watson from the pre-war days. Mabley had the money and Watson had the design. Barrie Price's father (his son is better known post-war for Lea Francis and Bugatti connections) had offered Mabley his factory in Kings Norton, Birmingham, to manufacture this post-war car, but it was too far away from London, where they wished to be based. In 1946 the Invicta Car Development Co. (London) Ltd was formed and premises were taken. The premises, on the London Road in Virginia Water, west of London and close to Staines, had been used by an aircraft assembly manufacturer during the war. After the Invicta period the premises became a well-known eating establishment – the Waterfall Restaurant.

The new Invicta model was named the Black Prince and the radiator was surmounted by a mascot in the image of a knight in armour, an emblem similar to that which had featured on the Invictas from the Fairmile. Press announcements were made at the end of 1946.

The new Invicta was an exceedingly high quality and luxurious vehicle, distinguished by a number of advanced technical features. A cruciform welded

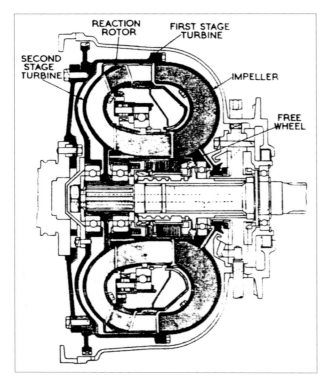

Left: The Brockhouse unit. A two-stage turbine dissipates the power at low forward speeds and becomes a locked form of transmission at 40mph. Inevitably, the power lost is released as heat into the atmosphere. (*Autocar*)

Below: The independent rear suspension consists of wishbones and a vertical guide system (see arrows). The rear brakes, being inboard, are sophisticated for a touring car. (*The Motor*)

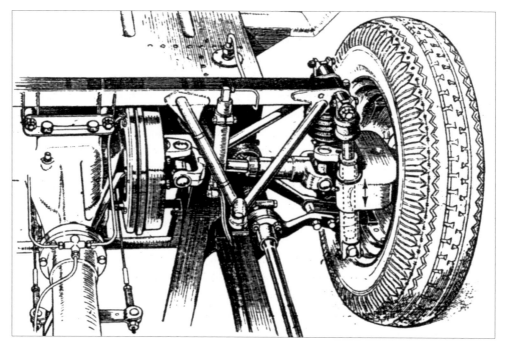

The independent front suspension again has a vertical guide with rack and pinion steering. The torsion bars are located midway down the chassis for front and rear suspension. (*The Motor*)

chassis was used, with independent suspension, front and rear, controlled by long torsion bars which ran along the side members and were attached halfway along the chassis. The engine was designed by William Watson with the assistance of two young men, who later joined Jaguar, and Watson oversaw the design of the complete car. The engine was built by Henry Meadows of Wolverhampton for the new Invicta company exclusively. It was a 2,997cc six-cylinder twin overhead camshaft unit developing 120bhp at 4,600rpm. It had wet liners, an alloy block, triple SU carburetters and an electric heater for the cylinder head, which was intended to be plugged into the owner's household mains supply. The most innovative feature of the Black Prince was the drive – the first British car with a fully automatic two-pedal transmission. In America automatic transmissions had been under development prior to the Americans entering the war and had received a major technical input with the applications for wartime use. Therefore, when Buick introduced the Buick Dynaflow in 1948, it was a tested form of drive. The Brockhouse Hydraulic Torque Converter (or 'turbotransmitter' as it was known) consisted of an automatically self-adjusting, infinitely variable geared transmission, operating as an oil-filled turbine, which converted the engine speed up to about 40mph when it worked like a normal fixed fluid coupling. There was the usual shaft drive to the rear axle, and the

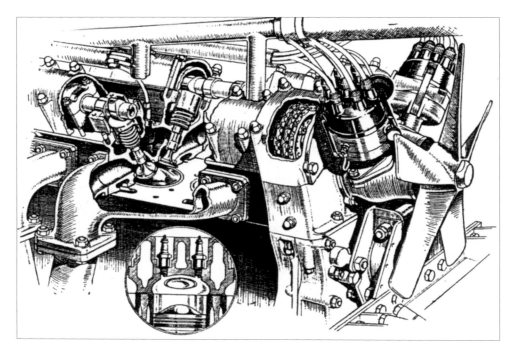

The twin overhead camshaft 3-litre engine has dual magneto and coil ignition with twin plugs per cylinder. Each camshaft is supported by twelve bearings. (*The Motor*)

epicyclic-operated reverse gear was selected by a switch on the dashboard. The only other controls were the accelerator and brake. The trouble with the Brockhouse was that it had not had any development. From 0–40mph, when the drive was direct, which was too wide a span without some stepped form of drive. The excess heat developed had to be lost to the atmosphere and was very obvious in low-speed town traffic.

There was the choice of Wentworth saloon or Byfleet drop-head coupe bodies, both of which were coachbuilt and were listed at a £2,300 basic price. With dry weight of 35 cwt and the peculiar form of transmission, acceleration was on the slow side away from a standing start, but it was obviously a fine car for high speed cruising. The prototype appeared in 1946, but development was slow and it was, in any case, an unfavourable time to market such an expensive car, as the Labour chancellor introduced double purchase tax for expensive cars. The price ex-works rose to £3,800 at the same time when a new Morris Minor was listed at £400. By the time the company was wound up in 1949, eighteen cars had been built. The majority of these have, since that time, been converted to a syncromesh gearbox (usually Jaguar). The turbotransmitter was not as foolproof as it the advertising had suggested, and it

The Invicta symbol, hand-painted and enamelled. It was said at the time that the designer, Watson, was influenced by effigies of the Black Prince at Canterbury.

The Byfleet drop-head coupe with the knight on the radiator cap. All Virginia Water cars were so equipped.

The prototype chassis on view in what is thought to be Rotterdam, in 1947.

is believed that the sole car left with this transmission is not a runner.

The company went up for sale. Mabley had lost £100,000 or more, and the other directors had also made losses proportional to their initial investment. The company assets were up for sale by auction and AFN Ltd, manufacturers of the Frazer Nash, bought items such as the marking-off table and the complete stocks of BSF cadmium-plated nuts and bolts. The auction was only partially successful and AFN Ltd subsequently bought the remainder and the company rights for a song.

If the car had been marketed with more conventional systems for the suspension and drive it might have survived, since the engine was very attractive and worked well. Too much untested innovation was too much.

APPENDIX TWO

THE S1 INVICTA FROM CHIPPENHAM, OCTOBER 2002

After the war there still remained a large quantity of spare parts for Invictas made by Macklin. This encouraged a new set of owners to become active with Invictas. Such people as Jack Marsh and Shutler took the S-Type and competed with them in Vintage Sports Car Club events. They worked on the cars themselves, quite often utilising the stock of spares in Flood Street which were sold off at near scrap prices. Jack Marsh, after several years, sold his 1930 S-Type to Michael Bristow. Bristow was extremely impressed with the all-round capabilities of the car (this vehicle had actually been the 'works' development car).

It was Andrew English, as motoring journalist for the *Daily Telegraph*, who spelt out in his press coverage of the launch of the new Invicta that 'if you want to make a small fortune building sports cars, start off with a large one'. It was at the 2002 British Motor Show, held at the National Exhibition Centre in Birmingham, that the new car was unveiled by Michael Bristow. The car, in recognition of the low chassis 4½-litre S-Type Invicta of 1930–31, was to be called the S1.

The S1 was aimed at the combined luxury GT and sports car market. Powered by a 320bhp ohc 4.6-litre V8 built by Ford, and driving through either an optional five-speed gearbox or an automatic with a limited slip differential (fitted as standard). It was anticipated that the S1 would be raced, but Michael Bristow has ruled out that option for his firm. However, the new company was going to support those who wish to go racing.

The press release photograph of the new S1 revealed at the 2002 British Motor Show.

The prototype about to be subject to wind tunnel testing. Note that subtle changes were made to the bodywork subsequent to this test.

The powerplant with the inlet manifold to the fuel injection, bearing the Invicta motif.

The S1 proudly showing off its lines.

The twelfth and thirteenth production Invictas in the course of construction.

The chassis, constructed of 50mm seamless high-tensile square tubing, supports the one-piece carbon composite bodyshell. The car was designed by Leigh Adams with the best components that could be brought together – in the same way as Bristow thought Noel Macklin had brought together the 1930 S-Type.

The price in 2002 was announced at £69,950 but by 2005 the price was over £100,000 due to the costs of the start-up and development. Michael Bristow said:

> The S1 is a thoroughly modern car, it fully embodies the standards, quality and spirit behind the race-winning 1930s Invicta cars. We are confident that it will provide today's motoring enthusiasts with an exceptionally rewarding driving and ownership experience, matching the marque's original promise to deliver the most wonderful performance in the world.

INDEX

Noel Macklin, the Cordery sisters and 'Cushie' Cushman occur frequently in the text and are not listed in this index. Neither are the appendices.

If you are interested in purchasing other books published by Tempus,
or in case you have difficulty finding any Tempus books in your local bookshop,
you can also place orders directly through our website

www.tempus-publishing.com